1/6/09

Dan Turpen (signature)

NOW WRITE!

Christmas, 2008
gift
from Mary & Audie Durfey

NOW WRITE!

Fiction Writing Exercises from Today's Best Writers and Teachers

Edited by SHERRY ELLIS

JEREMY P. TARCHER/PENGUIN

a member of Penguin Group (USA) Inc. · NEW YORK

JEREMY P. TARCHER/PENGUIN
Published by the Penguin Group
Penguin Group (USA) Inc., 375 Hudson Street, New York, New York 10014, USA •
Penguin Group (Canada), 90 Eglinton Avenue East, Suite 700, Toronto, Ontario
M4P 2Y3, Canada (a division of Pearson Penguin Canada Inc.) • Penguin Books Ltd,
80 Strand, London WC2R 0RL, England • Penguin Ireland, 25 St Stephen's Green,
Dublin 2, Ireland (a division of Penguin Books Ltd) • Penguin Group (Australia),
250 Camberwell Road, Camberwell, Victoria 3124, Australia (a division of Pearson
Australia Group Pty Ltd) • Penguin Books India Pvt Ltd, 11 Community Centre,
Panchsheel Park, New Delhi–110 017, India • Penguin Group (NZ), Cnr Airborne
and Rosedale Roads, Albany, Auckland 1310, New Zealand (a division of Pearson
New Zealand Ltd) • Penguin Books (South Africa) (Pty) Ltd, 24 Sturdee Avenue,
Rosebank, Johannesburg 2196, South Africa

Penguin Books Ltd, Registered Offices: 80 Strand, London WC2R 0RL, England

Most Tarcher/Penguin books are available at special quantity discounts for bulk
purchase for sales promotions, premiums, fund-raising, and educational needs.
Special books or book excerpts also can be created to fit specific needs. For details,
write Penguin Group (USA) Inc. Special Markets, 375 Hudson Street,
New York, NY 10014.

Library of Congress Cataloging-in-Publication Data

Now write! : fiction writing exercises from today's best writers and teachers / [compiled by] Sherry Ellis.
p. cm.
ISBN 1-58542-522-2
1. English language—Rhetoric—Problems, exercises, etc. 2. Creative writing—Problems, exercises, etc. 3. Fiction—Technique—Problems, exercises, etc.
I. Ellis, Sherry, date.
PE1413.N69   2006   2006045592
808.3—dc22

Printed in the United States of America
5 7 9 10 8 6 4

Book design by Gretchen Achilles

While the author has made every effort to provide accurate telephone numbers and
Internet addresses at the time of publication, neither the publisher nor the author
assumes any responsibility for errors, or for changes that occur after publication.
Further, the publisher does not have any control over and does not assume any
responsibility for author or third-party websites or their content.

CONTENTS

EDITOR'S NOTE   xi

GET WRITING!

Jayne Anne Phillips	Wedding Pictures	3
Robert Olen Butler	Through the Senses	5
Alison Lurie	My Pet	8
Alice Mattison	Two People Come Out of a Building and Into a Story	10
Alexander Chee	The Seed	12
Diana Abu-Jaber	Truthful Dare	16
Jill McCorkle	The Photograph	19
Rick Hillis	The Prefab Story Exercise	21
Maria Flook	The Upside-Down Bird: Hybridizing Memory, Place, and Invention	24
Paul Lisicky	A Map to Anywhere	31
Chuck Wachtel	Starting with the News	33
Debra Spark	Wedding Cake Assignment	36
Katherine A. Vaz	A Tabula Rasa Experiment	39
Karen Brennan	Collage	43
Dan Wakefield	The Five Senses	45
Crystal Wilkinson	Birth of a Story in an Hour or Less	47
Laurie Foos	Surrealism Exercise, or Thinking Outside the Box	52
Leslie Schwartz	Overcoming Dry Spells	54
Virgil Suárez	Field Trip	57

David Michael Kaplan   Smushing Seed Ideas Together   59

Kathleen Spivack   The Writing Exercise: A Recipe   63

POINT OF VIEW

Nina de Gramont   A Story to Tell   67

Maureen McCoy   First-Person Point of View: Imagining and Inhabiting Character   69

Clyde Edgerton   You-Me-I-You in the Cafeteria   71

Martha Cooley   Getting Characters' Ages Right   73

Paula Morris   What Are They Thinking? A Point-of-View Exercise   76

Daphne Kalotay   Third-Person Narration and "Psychic Distance"   78

Eileen Pollack   Look Backward, Angel   82

Laura Kasischke   Let the Dead Speak: An Exercise in First-Person Narration   84

CHARACTER DEVELOPMENT

Kay Sloan   Empathy and the Creation of Character   89

Michelle Herman   What's Under the Surface?   92

Lauren Grodstein   The Interview   96

Elizabeth Graver   "Once Upon a Time": Playing with Time in Fiction   99

Robert Anthony Siegel   Why I Stole It   103

Chris Abani   Language Portrait   105

Rachel Basch   Paw Through Their Pockets, Rifle Through Their Drawers: A Character Exercise   107

Maxine Chernoff   Mr. Samsa, Meet Bartleby   109

Michelle Brooks	Rattlesnake in the Drawer	112
K. L. Cook	A Family Theme, a Family Secret	114
Michael Datcher	Characters in Conflict	118
Edie Meidav	The Voyager: Write What You Don't Know: An Exercise in (Surprising Yourself with) Character	120
Joan Silber	Getting Dramatic	124
Mary Yukari Waters	Developing Your Characters	126
Lise Haines	The Way They Do the Things They Do	128
Cai Emmons	Braiding Time	132

DIALOGUE

Steven Schwartz	Snoop 'Da Dialogue	137
Sands Hall	Dialogue Without Words	139
Lon Otto	Hearing Voices	142
Thomas Fox Averill	Dialogue Exercise: The Non-Apology	145
Douglas Unger	Levels of Dialogue	148

PLOT AND PACING

Dan Chaon	Fictional Building Blocks	155
Renée Manfredi	Keep the Engine Running	158
Fred Leebron	The Riff	160
Brent Spencer	Storyboard Your Story	162
Sean Murphy and Tania Casselle	Sticking to the Structure	165
Kirby Gann	What Am I Writing About? Clarifying Story Ideas Through Summary	168

Douglas Bauer   The Richness of Resonance   171

SETTING AND DESCRIPTION

Margot Livesey   Setting in Fiction   175

Jim Heynen   The Character of Setting   177

Joan Leegant   Animating the Inanimate   179

Venise Berry   Learning to Layer   181

Patricia Powell   A Sense of Place   184

John Smolens   Be the Tree   186

Geoffrey Becker   A Very, Very Long Sentence   188

Karen E. Bender   Most Memorable Food:
                 Using Sensory Detail   190

Bret Anthony Johnston   Like Water for Words: A Simile Exercise   193

CRAFT

Susan Vreeland   Finding a Larger Truth by Turning
                 Autobiography into Fiction   199

Sheila Kohler   Secrets of the Great Scene   202

Tony Ardizzone   Hemingway's Caroms: Descriptive
                 Showing and Telling   206

Robert Boswell   How to Own a Story   208

Elizabeth Searle   Object Lessons   211

Rosellen Brown   The Goldilocks Method   214

Sandra Scofield   Big Scenes   218

Nancy Reisman   Moving Through Time:
                 A Four-Paragraph Short Short   221

Joy Passanante   Using the Retrospective Lens   224

Amy Bloom   Water Buddies   226

Victoria Redel	Listening to Sound to Find Sense	228
Lynne Barrett	Entrances: Building Bigger Scenes	230
Steve Almond	The Five Second Shortcut to Writing in the Lyric Register	233
Christopher Busa	Meaning Making Via Metaphor	235
Christopher Castellani	Soundtracking Your Story	239
Robert Cohen	Negative Capability	242

REVISION

Porter Shreve	Seven Drafts in Seven Days	247
Ann Harleman	More Is More: An Exercise in Revising Your Story	250
Brian Kiteley	Potholes	254
Jonis Agee	The Dark Matter: Twenty Issues in Novel Revision	257

AUTHOR WEB SITES 263

ACKNOWLEDGMENTS 265

CREDITS 267

EDITOR'S NOTE

When I decided to write a novel eight years ago, I didn't know how to learn the techniques and craft of writing fiction. Without the financial means or time to obtain an MFA, and without any prior writing courses under my belt, I decided to take a class at a community education program. I followed this up with private study with two writing coaches. To broaden my horizon, I attended mini-workshops and summer writing programs across the United States. Many of the teachers with whom I studied offered writing exercises as a means of advancing the study of craft and story. They often shared that they had used these exercises to help develop their own short stories and novels. *I loved these exercises!*

Inspired by my experience learning the craft of fiction writing, and having benefitted from writing exercises, I've collected the personal writing exercises of eighty-six novelists and short story writers. A veritable treasure trove of techniques, these exercises can jump-start the actual writing process, help you develop and deepen characters, get a handle on your plot and pacing, and even guide you in revision. Each exercise includes a brief commentary from the author, outlining the element of fiction writing their exercise addresses, and how the exercise helps them improve their own writing.

Now Write! is divided into eight sections that focus on: getting started, point of view, character development, dialogue, plot and pacing, setting and description, craft, and revision. These sections are organized in the order in which an aspiring writer might approach her work—getting the words out first, then honing the various elements of a work of fiction, including the all-important revisions. Go ahead: *Now write!*

GET WRITING!

WEDDING PICTURES

Jayne Anne Phillips is the author of three novels, *Machine Dreams*, *Shelter*, and *MotherKind*, and two widely anthologized story collections, *Black Tickets* and *Fast Lanes*. She is the recipient of the Sue Kaufman Prize for First Fiction, an Academy Award in Literature from the American Academy and Institute of Arts and Letters, a Guggenheim Fellowship, two National Endowment for the Arts Fellowships, a Bunting Fellowship from the Bunting Institute of Radcliffe College, and a Howard Foundation Fellowship. Her work has appeared in *Harper's*, *Granta*, *Doubletake*, *The Southern Review*, and *The Norton Anthology of Contemporary Fiction*. She has taught at Harvard University, Williams College, Brandeis University, and Boston University. She is currently a professor of English at Rutgers-Newark University, where she will design and direct a new MFA Program. She lives in Boston and New York.

My first publication was *Sweethearts*, a fine arts limited edition of 500 copies published by Truck Press under the editorship of David Wilk in Carrboro, North Carolina. (My thanks to David Southern for the beautiful design evident on the cover and throughout *Sweethearts*.) The cover of the book featured my parents' wedding picture—one reason my (divorced) mother kept her copy of *Sweethearts* in the piano bench. But it's a beautiful photograph, with the same dark layerings all wedding pictures possess.

EXERCISE

The Wedding Picture exercise can be an evocative one-page fiction assignment. The exercise is to ask students to color copy their own wedding photograph, that of their parents, or an anonymous wedding picture, and to write a one-page fiction inspired by the image, with "Wedding Picture" as an example. My classes have sometimes made their "Wedding Picture" exercises into chapbooks entitled "Class Pictures."

SWEETHEARTS
JAYNE ANNE PHILLIPS

WEDDING PICTURE

My mother's ankles curve from the hem of a white suit as if the bones were water. Under the cloth her body in its olive skin unfolds. The black hair, the porcelain neck, the red mouth that barely shows its teeth. My mother's eyes are round and wide as a light behind her skin burns them to coals. Her heart makes a sound that no one hears. The sound says each fetus floats, an island in the womb.

My father stands beside her in his brown suit and two-tone shoes. He stands also by the plane in New Guinea in 1944. On its side there is a girl on a swing wearing spike heels and short shorts. Her breasts balloon; the sky opens inside them. Yellow hair smooth as a cats, she is swinging out to him. He glimmers, blinded by the light. Now his big fingers curl inward. He is trying to hold something.

In her hands the snowy Bible hums, nuns swarming a honeyed cell. The husband is an afterthought. Five years since the highschool lover crumpled on the bathroom floor, his sweet heart raw. She's twenty-three, her mother's sick, it's time. My father's heart pounds, a bell in a wrestler's chest. He is almost forty and the lilies are trumpeting. Rising from his shoulders, the cross grows pale and loses its arms in their heads.

THROUGH THE SENSES

Robert Olen Butler specializes in fiction and screenwriting. He is the author of ten novels and three collections of stories. In addition to winning a Pulitzer Prize in 1993 for his story collection, *A Good Scent from a Strange Mountain*, he won a National Magazine Award in 2001. He has received a Guggenheim Fellowship in fiction, a National Endowment for the Arts grant, as well as the Richard and Hinda Rosenthal Award from the American Academy of Arts and Letters. His other most famous books include: *The Alleys of Eden, Tabloid Dreams, The Deep Green Sea*, and *Had a Good Time*. His stories have appeared in *The New Yorker, Esquire, The Paris Review, The Sewanee Review, The Best American Short Stories, New Stories from the South*, and many other journals. He holds a distinguished Frances Eppes Professorship at Florida State University.

This is a coached writing exercise in seven stages from my book of lectures *From Where You Dream*. **Do each stage separately.** Make certain you've finished a stage before you move on to the next one.

Use no abstraction, no generalization, no summary, no analysis, no interpretation. Force yourself to write moment to moment through the senses only. Don't hassle your style at this point, don't agonize over just the right word; just keep the flow of it through the senses—flowing, flowing, flowing. Don't think, don't think. Senses, senses, senses. If you really do that rigorously you'll find yourself flowing right down—at least into the foyer of—this great house that is your unconscious.

I want you to write in the first person. When I say "you" I am referring to your character.

Now, about the character. If you have a character you've been working with closely, you may write from the viewpoint of that character, but I'm reluctant to encourage this, because then the exercise will not be very useful to you. In the absence of any character you have a desperate need to get back in touch with, I urge you to write through a character with demographics very similar to your own. This is not you, it is not autobiography, but unless you've got a really burning character that you need to explore, then the character you choose needs to be very close to you in age, gender, ethnicity and so forth.

Important: **Do Not Read Ahead**. Take each step one at a time and let the next step surprise you.

EXERCISE

Step One

You awake abruptly, though it isn't morning, and you're not in a bed. But you are in the place where you live. The room where you awake is right in objects and their associations. You are breathless and anxious from a dream you can't, and won't, remember. You look around the room, everything in it is shaped by an unspecified anxiety. Let's see the room, in the moment, through the senses.

Step Two

One object in particular catches your attention and suggests a strong connection to your anxiety. Move toward that object; touch it, experience it sensually.

Step Three

The object evokes a memory as vivid as a dream but not the one you woke from. It is a real memory, one based on wanting, desiring something. But this is a surface thing you want—an object, a gesture, a touch, whatever. Focus on the moment-to-moment, specific memory of desiring this thing, which, nevertheless, carries an intimation of deeper yearning. But don't go to that deeper desire yet. Experience the surface thing through just your character's sensibility.

Step Four

Now let the memory of this want include a moment when a second memory is evoked. This second memory involves another object, different from the one you are touching in the present time but similar to it in its basic sensual pattern. This second memory surprises you. You deeply connect it to the first. And the *wanting* suddenly goes deeper, into a state of being, a state of self. Don't label it. Play it out in the moment through the senses.

Step Five

In that second memory you are moved to an action driven by your yearning. Let the action happen moment to moment.

Step Six

Some part of the action will bring you back to the present, to an awareness of the first object. Re-experience your object. Your sensual perception of it is altered, is reshaped by the emotion and yearning you have experienced in these two linked memories.

Step Seven

Now, back in the present, in the light of all this, you take an action.

ALISON LURIE

MY PET

Alison Lurie is the 1984 Pulitzer Prize–winning author of *Foreign Affairs*. She is also the author of nine other novels: *Love and Friendship, The Nowhere City, Imaginary Friends, Real People, The War Between the Tates, Only Children, The Truth About Lorin Jones, The Last Resort*, and *Truth and Consequences*, her newest work. She has also written a collection of ghost stories, three collections of folktales for children, a collection of essays on children's literature and folklore, a memoir, and a book on the psychology of fashion. Her work has been translated into twelve languages. Since 1970 she has taught literature, folklore, and writing at Cornell University.

EXERCISE

Write a composition on the subject "My Pet." The only requirement is that this must be a pet you have never owned. It can be anything from a kitten to a dinosaur, from a fly to a dragon. Describe what your pet looks like, how you acquired it, what it eats and where it sleeps, what tricks it can do, and how it gets on with your family, friends, neighbors, and/or the people at work.

    We are, we are told, a nation of pet lovers, and more than that, half the households in America include an animal, bird, or fish. What are the motives for keeping a pet? Possible suggestions are: need for protection, need for affection (a creature you can love and/

or one that will love you), aesthetic pleasure (the beautiful pet, the pet as interior decoration or status symbol), parental feeling (a child substitute), sadistic impulses (something to maltreat), etc. What is the function of the pet in your exercise?

A portrait of a pet is also one way of creating a portrait of its owner. What does this exercise tell us about the pet's owner (for instance, that he is kind, timid, affectionate, loves beauty, etc.)?

It has also often been remarked that some people come to resemble their pets or vice versa. Why does this happen? In other cases, the pet is extremely different from the owner; possibly it may express impulses that its owner does not want to or cannot express (for example, the actively aggressive dog with an apparently passive and peaceful owner). Is the pet in your composition like or unlike its owner and how?

ALICE MATTISON

TWO PEOPLE COME OUT OF A BUILDING AND INTO A STORY

Alice Mattison's newest work is her collection of connected stories, *In Case We're Separated*. Her most recent novel is *The Wedding
of the Two-Headed Woman;* her earlier books of fiction include *The
Book Borrower* and *Men Giving Money, Women Yelling*, both New
York Times Notable Books. Her stories, essays, and poems have appeared in *The New Yorker, Ploughshares, The Threepenny Review,
AGNI, Shenandoah,* and in many other journals, and have been anthologized in *The Best American Short Stories* and *The Pushcart
Prize*. She teaches fiction in the Bennington MFA program.

The only exercise I know is one I don't use much myself because it works a little *too* well. It can feel extremely compelling. It's useful if you're trying to discover what to write
next, and are willing to be surprised. Say to yourself, "Two people
are coming out of a building."

Stories are inside us waiting to be written. We may not know
what they are, but we know *something*. If someone tells you—or you
tell yourself—that two people are coming out of a building, you'll
find you know something, right away, about those two people. You
won't make decisions about them; you'll see them in your mind's
eye. Maybe one is wearing a hat. Maybe one is laughing. When you

ask questions about them, answers will slowly come. You must be patient and receptive.

Ask questions like, Are they relieved or sorry to be coming out of the building? Are they about to separate or go somewhere together? Are they men, women, children? Are they new acquaintances or people who know each other well? You may not know for a while exactly how they are connected, but I suspect you will know pretty readily the degree of connection; you'll know (as you might, watching strangers in the street) whether they've just met or know each other well, whether they're happy to be in each other's company or not. Only later will you realize that they are a lawyer and client, a mother and daughter, a teacher and student, two brothers.

If you find you're making decisions instead of observing, slow down. Keep asking questions. Trust your answers if they feel true, even if they seem strange—especially if they seem strange. Is this building a house, a store, an office building? And where are they going next? Once you know not just the feel of where they are going, but where they are actually going—a cemetery, a school, a bank—you can ask the next question. What will happen there—what *could* happen there? And what might happen after that? When you actually write the story, the two people may not come out of the building at the beginning. They may come out in the middle or at the end, or maybe they won't come out of the building in this story at all; maybe the story will be about what happened to them before they went into the building, or inside it, or what happened the next day or week or year.

ALEXANDER CHEE

THE SEED

Alexander Chee is the author of the novels *Edinburgh* and *The Queen of the Night*, forthcoming from Houghton Mifflin in the fall of 2007. He is the recipient of the Whiting Award and the National Endowment for the Arts Fellowship in Literature. His stories and essays have appeared in the anthologies *Men on Men 2000*, *Boys Like Us*, *Loss Within Loss*, and *The M Word*. He has taught fiction- and nonfiction-writing workshops at Wesleyan University and The New School in New York City. He lives in Maine.

Write brief descriptions of three early childhood stories that have been told to you about yourself, but that you, on hearing the story, had no actual memories of. Stories told to you by relatives or family friends.

Look at them. Can you see the events? If so, how did you get the visual memory? Contrast these with the memory you have of a more important event in your life, a contemporary event. What distinguishes them?

Can you see how the "memory" you have of the early childhood story is likely an animation of album photos?

When I was two, I had the habit of hiding behind furniture and imitating the voices of adults in the room. There was one time when my grandmother and her daughter, my young, high-school-age aunt, were fighting. They were arguing in Korean and I began imitating what each of them said. They paused, stunned. My grandmother began laughing but my aunt became enraged, and from what I can tell may still be angry at me for this.

I can "see" the event but I am wearing something I know I wore then from the pictures that exist of me from the time, and my idea of the room is colored by the pictures of the room that exist and the memories I have of being in that room later, as an adult. I can look at a child-size me, with his overalls, side-part hair and close-lipped smile. And as he comes out of hiding, he is not me, but a character based on myself, invented by me, to illustrate something I have heard about myself and also know to be true: I am still a mimic.

This is, in other words, an early autobiographical fiction. These stories are told to us by people trying to tell us something about ourselves. The idea is that through these stories we have access to an early and unconscious self, an identity that is somehow original to us. The irony is that we receive it indirectly but can experience it directly. Some of us are even controlled by these early stories of ourselves—friends and family may use them to remind us of who they think we are well after we move on from them. Either way, they factor into our sense of identity. And this is why they are useful to a fiction writer.

Back during the writing of my first novel, I took up a conscious way of writing autobiographical fiction because I saw in workshops that the unconscious way I was working left me with too few answers about what I was making. And too little control. My teacher at the time was Marilynne Robinson, at Iowa, and she was telling us regularly about talking to our unconscious minds, about making writing a way to tap into that. This exercise comes out of that urging.

I could use this story of myself then to write a story about a character who is a mimic. The conflict of the whole story is set there also, ready-made: the grandmother is an early ally, and the aunt, an early antagonist. I am a small child, but this doesn't make me less threatening to the teenager aunt, but more so: I am uncomplicated, I win her mother's love easily and apparently by making fun of her. I am an easy enemy for her. She is too young to understand that I don't do this consciously.

The grandmother reacts the way she does because I am the child of her favorite son. She has always allowed her son a certain amount of mischief because he has learned to defy her in ways that still win her love. None of the rest of her children will learn this.

Using this allows me to begin with an event that has its own power to convey meaning, a situation with tension. From the beginning, something is happening, a friction point that is a crucial matter to the beginnings of fiction. This is not about how the young child "feels." It is about a child learning the power and danger of a gift he can use but cannot understand, and his life is going to be shaped by his experiments with it and the reactions he provokes. This moment is the first time he uses it, and the power relationships between him, his aunt and his grandmother shift as a result. Their relationships to each other will never be the same. Afterward, the aunt will feel unloved for no reason. The grandson will feel loved for no reason. And the grandmother will not explain herself. She will not see the problem, only thinking her daughter has no sense of humor, and her grandson, a born charmer.

One thing a fiction is is a situation as it moves through time, and the relationships of the people in that situation to each other and to the situation

EXERCISE

Look at your three moments. Pick one that is the most interesting to you. Answer these questions: 1. What is the situation of this memory? Be more precise. Think of economic factors, social factors. 2. What are the motives of the people involved, including the self-character? 3. What are their power-relations? 4. What can be changed? Can the setting be changed? Can an aunt be an uncle, a grandmother, a teacher? How can you further displace the identities of the people involved in ways that allow you to turn them into characters but to also retain the potential emotional arc and your sympathy for it?

Now, write a fuller description of the scene having thought through all of these answers, and see where it goes.

TRUTHFUL DARE

Diana Abu-Jaber's novel *Crescent* has been translated into nine languages and won the PEN Center Award for Literary Fiction and the Before Columbus Foundation American Book Award. It was also named a Notable Book of the Year by *The Christian Science Monitor*. Her first novel, *Arabian Jazz*, won the Oregon Book Award in 1994. Her newest book is a food memoir entitled *The Language of Baklava* and was a Borders Original Voices selection. Her work has also appeared in such publications as *The New York Times*, *Ms.*, *Salon*, *Gourmet*, *Good Housekeeping*, and *The Nation*. She has taught at a number of universities, including the University of Michigan, the University of Oregon, UCLA, and the University of Miami. She is currently writer-in-residence at Portland State University.

I love exercises that help writers to limber up and get their creative juices flowing. To a certain extent, I think that all timed "free writing" exercises can help with this process. By making yourself write quickly, without stopping, within a certain time limit, you can push yourself beyond everyday constraint and habit into new areas of discovery.

In addition, by assigning yourself themes, topics, and directions in timed writing, you can help hone specific areas of craft, including character development, dialogue, setting, among many others.

One of my favorite timed writing exercises helps push you toward achieving emotional bravery in your writing.

EXERCISE

The assignment is very simple: Write about how you first learned about sex.

Give yourself about a half hour to write very quickly, without stopping, about your earliest memory of sexual discovery. Dare yourself to be as honest as you can be. There is no one right way to do this exercise. For some, this assignment might produce very humorous work, for others it might be embarrassing, or heartbreaking. Possibly, all the above.

In general terms, the relative success or failure of an exercise like this will depend on how much emotional honesty you're able to bring to your writing. Writing is one of the first and best places for us to find shared truth and meaning, stripped of posturing and pretension. If we agree with Kafka's assessment that writing gives us an "axe for the frozen sea within," then the ability to write well and convincingly about one's own sexuality can be the ultimate challenge and liberation.

Many writers have told me, over the years, that they could never write about this or that experience due to the fear that someone they know might read about it and be offended. We are often our own greatest censors, stopping ourselves from writing our stories before anyone else has a chance to try. If you have trouble with this exercise, you may find that you'll want to return to it and try it at different times to see what sorts of stories emerge. This exercise encourages us to "own" our own experiences. We all have a right to our own stories and our private interpretations of events—no matter how differently others might see them.

For that reason, this exercise is helpful whether you're interested in writing fiction or nonfiction. It can help memoirists get in touch with important memories, and help novelists to deepen their characters. In either case, it also seems to be very good at helping writers start to develop their own voices, and it reminds us that we really do have lots of stories all our own. When you get stuck for ideas, re-invoking your own early adventures and discoveries can be a great source of inspiration. If you approach this exercise with boldness, bravery, and a bit of audacity (remind yourself that you can always burn the exercise later . . . if you really want to), you, like many writers, may discover that you possess an innate sense of humor and charm or bravery or inventiveness that you never before recognized. And that's always a good thing.

THE PHOTOGRAPH

Jill McCorkle is the author of three short story collections, *Crash Diet: Stories, Final Vinyl Days*, and most recently *Creatures of Habit*; and five novels, *The Cheer Leader, July 7th, Tending to Virginia, Ferris Beach*, and *Carolina Moon*. Five of her books have been selected as New York Times Notable Books of the Year. Her stories have appeared in *The Atlantic Monthly, Bomb, Cosmopolitan, Ladies' Home Journal*, and *Ploughshares*. "Billy Goats" appeared in *The Best American Short Stories 2002*. She has taught at the University of North Carolina at Chapel Hill, Harvard University, and Brandeis University and currently teaches in the Bennington MFA Program. She lives near Boston with her two children.

I think for me as a writer, one of the most difficult tasks is eliminating the material that takes me in a million different directions. When I have a student with the problem (a good problem!) of too many ideas racing forward at once, I first suggest an exercise to clean out the attic—an exercise that my college professor Max Steele handed out which is to set aside a thirty-minute block of time and write a one-thousand-word sentence. No need to pay attention to structure or punctuation; no need to edit. Just begin writing and let it go. Once all the ideas are out there on the page, it is easier to pick something in particular, which is where my chosen exercise comes in.

EXERCISE

Pick an image. This can be a photograph from your personal life, a picture in a magazine or in an art gallery or it can be part of a memory, a stilled image, real or imagined. What is important is that you have in your mind a picture that is framed—isolated if you will—from everything else. This frame serves as the structure of the story; you are bound to what lies within. And yet, there is so much more within than meets the eye. You can describe what is there, but you also have the power to imagine what happened just prior to this event. How did this image come to be? And you have the power to project what might happen next. The focus is still on the particular present and yet, doors and windows fly open on either side, broadening the history and knowledge. This is an exercise I use often when wanting to sharpen or focus a scene.

THE PREFAB STORY EXERCISE

Rick Hillis has published a book of short stories, *Limbo River*, a collection of poems, *The Blue Machines of Night*, and has worked in screenwriting. He has taught fiction, poetry, and screenwriting at a number of institutions, including DePauw University in Greencastle, Indiana, where he now makes his home.

To be honest, I don't assign many exercises. Actually, the Four Page Traditional Story is about it. Perhaps this is because I didn't take undergraduate creative-writing workshops and so was never exposed to exercises. I do understand the value of exercises, though, and the students' need for them, but for better or for worse, I like to get to the real thing as soon as possible.

The Four Page Traditional Story, to me, is both exercise and the real thing. I usually assign it—or a variation of it—to intro classes very early in the semester and give the students no more than a couple of days to write it. In workshop, we focus on the elements of fiction, going through them almost one by one. Within about four classes we're ready to move on. The students have composed a story (in several cases, their best of the semester—whether they know it or not) and are familiar with the workshop method and the language of appreciating fiction, and the exercise has served a great purpose.

The beauty of the prefab story exercise is twofold: any or all of the elements that play a part in short stories can be emphasized, and in the end the student has a completed story. Often, in my intro-to-fiction workshops, these prefab stories are among the strongest and most memorable of the semester.

EXERCISE

Here are the guidelines:

1. The story will be between three and five pages. No longer.

2. The action happens over a long weekend.

3. The story opens with a line of exposition as the protagonist watches the antagonist arrive.

4. The antagonist has something that the protagonist wants or thinks he or she deserves.

5. Over the course of the weekend, the protagonist is presented with the opportunity of taking this object of desire . . . or not.

6. Important, this "thing" should have metaphorical suggestiveness. It should be the controlling metaphor and the title of the story.

7. As important, nothing is explained; we are told nothing or almost nothing. Everything—meaning, feeling, thought—unfolds through action, detail, description.

That's it—a basic "who's that knocking on my door" story. I should warn you that some creative students may balk at this exercise because it at first seems that all of the creative choices have been removed. Not true. The guidelines merely control time, and insist on the traditional storytelling fundamentals: conflict, action, and metaphor. The most important choices are up to the student. Is the setting at a cabin at a summer camp or a construction site? Does the antagonist arrive in a horse-drawn buggy or a Cadillac? Is the narrator a kid or an adult? What's the point of view? What holiday is it?—Easter, Christmas, Thanksgiving? Is the "thing" a bowling trophy (probably a comic tone) or a hearing aid that is not only the source of your cousin's sudden popularity, but seems to pick up messages from dead Aunt Ruby? (probably not a comic tone). Although it does not strictly follow the prefab rules (and I always allow students to break the rules to make a stronger story), Raymond Carver's "Viewfinder" works as model.

A variation of this exercise that is perhaps easier for students to get excited about is the basic "road trip" strategy. In this case, the protagonist will be on a trip to a funeral, reunion, birthday party, hockey game, concert . . . and will encounter—within the first paragraph—someone or something that changes the direction of the story. As with "who's knocking at my door," it may be helpful if this someone possesses something (tangible is always best) that the protagonist wants, needs, will sacrifice common sense to get. In the end, this encounter changes the protagonist's life if only in a minute way. This version works well when stressing setting, sensory detail, and action; it helps students avoid the pitfall of writing a static story

MARIA FLOOK

THE UPSIDE-DOWN BIRD: HYBRIDIZING MEMORY, PLACE, AND INVENTION

Maria Flook is a novelist and nonfiction writer. Her books include the novels *Lux*, *Open Water*, and *Family Night*; the story collection *You Have the Wrong Man*; and the nonfiction books *Invisible Eden: A Story of Love and Murder on Cape Cod* and *My Sister Life: The Story of My Sister's Disappearance*. She is writer in residence at Emerson College.

I once went to look at "Twelve, Twelve," the house where I grew up as a child. My family had long ago splintered apart and my parents had moved out. I had my two children with me when I drove into my old neighborhood in a suburb of Wilmington, Delaware, "the Chemical Capital of the World."

My teenage daughter and my young son, who was still in a stroller, didn't understand my mix of pounding sentiment and anxiety, the secret pull I felt to return to that cracked, flagstone stoop. I wanted to ring the doorbell at "Twelve, Twelve" and ask the current residents if I could poke around outside. Secretly, I had hoped that I might be invited to come inside again. I wanted to show my kids a little French tile cemented to the fireplace mantel. The tile has haunted and intrigued me since I left it behind years ago. Its design was a painted bird—flying upside down! The upside-down bird was a mistake—but to me, it was charmed.

The tile seemed to represent my earliest conscious entry into the kind of life I live today.

If the tile hadn't been removed by the new owners of the house, I wanted to ask them if I might reclaim it. A stone mason could chisel it loose and repair the mantel. I'd offer to pay for the job.

But everything went wrong.

To begin with, when I drove to my house in Woodside Hills, the familiar, pastoral road that had once fed into my neighborhood was closed. Backhoes, earth movers, and New Jersey barricades made it impossible to approach the house. They were building one of those huge "Box Stores," a Wal-Mart or Home Depot—and traffic was diverted. But then I saw a sign announcing the project. The "Big Box" store was actually going to be a new mini max complex for the Delaware Dept. of Corrections.

I had to backtrack a few miles and circle around the construction site. The detour brought me past my old high school which was boarded up with plywood. Its white brick shell had elaborate gang tags scrolling across it. The empty structure was so ornately decorated with furious bright-colored messaging that it looked like a kind of Hip Hop Fabergé egg. I eventually entered my neighborhood from a declining part of town that seemed to have evolved into an entirely different demographic from the white middle class it had been twenty-five years ago. Just two blocks from my home, a methadone clinic was in full operation with long queues of patient souls waiting on the sidewalk. The house next door to the clinic was where I had often played with my classmate Betty Diggs, trading clothes for our Barbie dolls. Betty's place was now a "Plasma Center" where addicts from the methadone clinic could sell their plasma for a few bucks.

But when I reached my own street it looked familiar enough, although embowered with mature arborvitae. Hedges that once had been merely waist high now tipped into rooftops. I parked before my old house, a long fieldstone ranch. When my kids and I got out of the car to look at the place, I saw that every single window shade was drawn down to the sills. The windows were opaque. You could no longer see into the living room through the massive picture window, a huge, open rectangle that was so common to the fifties' trophy house ideal. But even the big window had been sealed with a vinyl sheet. There was no way to peek into the interior, or to see the little upside-down bird perched on the fireplace.

At the front door, with my kids beside me, I tried the doorbell. But when I pushed the little white plastic button, the doorbell exploded! The little spring inside the mechanism launched full force, shooting the button off and stinging my breastbone. After decades of service, the device quit there and then, shooting me point-blank, as if in warning.

I used the knocker. No one answered. My mother would have come to the door in her glamorous lounge pajamas, but the current couple must have both worked. No "stay at home moms" these days, I thought. There was no glamour puss matriarch like my mother who had often spritzed herself with Joy Patou to greet salesmen and dry cleaners. When I knocked once again, I thought I saw the vinyl wall shiver against the picture window, as if someone had tried to get a peek at me.

I turned my children around and we started to walk away when the front door opened a crack. I saw only a wedge of black, but no one had appeared.

"Excuse me?" I said. "I don't mean to bother you—"

"Then go away," a voice said.

"Well, okay," I said. "I just wanted to see the old place."

The door didn't budge, but I saw the hand on the doorknob, a woman's slender fingers beneath the cuff of her terry bathrobe.

"That little bird on the mantel?" I said. "I'd love to see it."

"Get lost." The door swept shut.

I put my son in the stroller, and because of the rude exchange, I decided I'd ignore the inhospitable crone who had begged off her hostess duties and take my kids around the house to see the gardens. The shrubs were sofa-sized when once it had been my chore to stand with a garden hose above the diminutive ewes and hy-drangeas my father had planted. As I told my daughter some of the Latin names for the flowers my father had nurtured, I noticed the lone homebody watched us from window to window. I waved at her once or twice, but each time she stepped away.

Next, I found the bank of sunken garbage pails outside the kitchen door, strange metal cylinders that opened with a foot pedal. I explained to my children that before my sister had run away from home, we had often climbed inside these tombs when playing hide and seek. My daughter wondered how we had had the nerve to sink into the smelly crypts. "You played in these garbage cans? No won-der she ran away."

"We were kids," I said. It was youth that gave us the noncha-lance to climb into underground trash bins. When I tried to pry them open now, I discovered that the lids had been welded shut.

"For safety's sake," my daughter said.

I wanted to show my kids the rest of the neighborhood and we pushed the stroller up the street to visit the old skating pond. The idyllic pond was where we had played ice hockey in the winter and where, in summer, we counted water lilies that floated like cracked white china saucers. We had liked to find our reflections in the still water—our faces surrounded by blossoms. But the beloved reflect-ing pool had been filled in. It was a tennis court now, its surface cov-ered in a cracked green rubber coating. The tennis court was in ill repair, and the house itself, once a manse, looked seedy, like the va-cant façade in Cheever's story "The Swimmer."

A man stood in his doorway with his arms crossed. His expres-sion: Get Lost!

Another face appeared next door. Ditto!

I was ready to go. I suddenly understood that I wasn't supposed to be there. I recounted to my daughter what had happened that day. One, I couldn't drive straight home on the usual route, but was forced to find a detour. Two, the windows of my home were ob-scured. Three, the doorbell exploded! Four, we couldn't find our faces in the little reflective pond of my childhood. These metaphors were glaring, and I tried to get some sympathy from my kids. My daughter said, "Right. So can we leave now?" My son drummed his heels in his cage on wheels.

I knew someday they'd have their own stories.

As we were ready to pile back into the car where we had left it parked in front of "Twelve, Twelve," the mystery woman inside stepped out onto the stoop. She circled her arm. "I guess you can come see it," she said.

I trotted ahead of my daughter who tried to lug her two-year-old brother after me. The woman led us into the living room. It was a mess. Filmed wineglasses, plates of untouched dinners, haystacks of dried spaghetti, maybe a week's worth of microwaved entrees and half-eaten English muffins were deposited on every available surface. Newspapers were spread across the floor as if someone was trying to housetrain a puppy. The untidy scene was instantly familiar. A domestic melodrama was in its second act and its very private squalor was not as repellant to me as it was sympathetic. Something horrible had happened—a tragedy not unlike the many that these rooms had been steeped in before. It was my mess as much as hers, I thought.

The woman, about forty years old, sank into a chair and held her palm across her forehead, as if she had a terrible headache,

Migraine, I thought. That explains the bathrobe, the messy house.

But she said, "He left a week ago. I've been less than normal since—sorry." She tipped her face to look at me standing in the center of her aftermath, as if she wished I could assume some of its burden. She seemed to sense my willingness to adapt to it.

"I'm so sorry," I said.

"It was coming, I shouldn't have been shocked. But—"

My daughter had wandered into the room with my son. My daughter didn't wriggle her nose or lift her chin as she surveyed the destroyed living room. She had heard a lot about that house from *me,* and didn't seem surprised to see its perpetual squalor. She had quite a lot of poise for a girl on the brink of the mean teens, and maybe she'd be spared what she sees here.

"Well, there it is, I guess," the woman said, pointing to the fireplace.

I walked up to the mantel to look at the upside-down bird.

The tile was brightly painted, with all its original charm, but I was more inclined to examine the photographs propped along the mantel. There were pictures of the bedraggled woman with her husband in happier times. Their wedding day. A picnic. A Christmas tree with two little kids crouched before a pyramid of gifts. And a recent snapshot of the couple at midlife, snuggled together on the bow of a small sailboat, wrapped in a Hudson Bay blanket.

The woman said, "That stupid little bird. It's a joke." She could have been referring to her husband's mistress or to herself.

"A lucky mistake," I said. "That's what my mother called it."

"Oh, don't get me wrong. I like it. It grows on you after a while."

"Yes. It's a great little tile." I knew I wasn't going to ask for it back.

We piled back into the car. I felt guilty to abandon the betrayed housewife in her time of need, but I left my old neighborhood. As we backtracked past the Plasma Center and the methadone clinic, we realized that we'd forgotten the baby stroller on the sidewalk when we had strapped the toddler in his car seat. I had to circle back to retrieve it. But the stroller wasn't on the shoulder of the road where we had left it. I believed that the mournful housewife had brought it inside to save it for me. But when I knocked, no one answered the door. The heartbroken hostess had swiped the stroller and she herself had evaporated in less than five minutes. From an open window, I thought I heard the woman finally loading her dishwasher—or the little upside-down bird singing in tinkling, ceramic notes.

EXERCISE

The sample above is both a true story, with factual details, and one of vivid invention. Write a brief five-page story about a character returning to her childhood house or apartment, or perhaps to the place where she lived with her first husband or lover. Retrieve from true memory the setting, and the meaningful history it has to the subject. Invent what might happen when the character returns—who will answer the door—what might the character want to get from the new occupant? What conflict emerges from this meeting? What insights or analysis of self erupts from a detour into past experience melded with a journey into current worlds? Invent new details to enforce the historical triggers. As Matisse said, "Exaggerate in the direction of truth." Harvest characters from the narrator's past but introduce and juxtapose new characters in order to explore the main character's complexity. What were the conditions in her past residence and what are her current conflicts—how does history inform the present? How does "sense of place" adhere to the psychological landscape? What brings her back to that address, or chases her away? You can have great instants of action, absurd observation, and dialogue between strangers or old acquaintances.

Examine what is at stake.

A MAP TO ANYWHERE

Paul Lisicky is the author of *Lawnboy* and *Famous Builder.* His work has appeared in *Ploughshares, Prairie Schooner, Short Takes, Open House,* and in other magazines and anthologies. His awards include fellowships from the National Endowment for the Arts, the James Michener/Copernicus Society, and the Fine Arts Work Center in Provincetown, Massachusetts, where he was twice a Winter Fellow. He teaches at Sarah Lawrence College and lives in New York City. He recently completed *Lumina Harbor,* a novel.

Why are *you* writing this story?

There comes a point in the life of many narratives where it helps to think about this question. Not that there should necessarily be any direct correlation between invention and autobiography, but any fiction writer needs to engage the stuff of his own real-life predicaments in order to write work that's strange and alive. I suggest the following exercise for stories (or novels!) that strike you as competent but tidy, dull, or inert. At the very least you'll have a clearer sense of why the tale matters to you, so you'll be able to crack it open on an emotional level. You'll also come to a stronger understanding of the power of setting and individual perception, and the interrelationship between the two.

EXERCISE

1. Take a piece of paper and use the whole sheet to draw the map of a meaningful landscape—e.g., a neighborhood, a park, an empty lot—from your childhood. Take twenty minutes and fill in as many specific details as you can.

2. Mark the location of three significant incidents on the map.

3. Imagine yourself into one of those incidents and write a list of sensory details (sound, smell, etc.) you associate with the experience.

4. Using the most evocative details on your list, write the incident as a two-page scene.

5. Finally, write another version of the scene reimagining the experience from the point of view of your central character.

STARTING WITH THE NEWS

Chuck Wachtel is the author of the novels *Joe the Engineer*, winner of the PEN/Hemingway Citation, and *The Gates*; a collection of stories and novellas, *Because We Are Here* (all from Viking/Penguin USA); and five collections of poems and short prose, including *The Coriolis Effect* and, most recently, *What Happens to Me*. He has taught at Skidmore College, Sarah Lawrence College, Purdue University, and in the MFA Program for Writers at Warren Wilson College. He currently teaches in the Graduate Program in Creative Writing at NYU.

Beginning a story or longer work of fiction is the act of building an entrance before walking through it, and for the writer the process begins even before the first word is written: with an encounter with the kernel of a resonant narrative idea: a memory, an image, an observation, an overheard phrase, an event, a fragment of a dream. More important than the source is that the subject you choose, or that chooses you, strikes you as possessed of meaning and possibility.

EXERCISE

An exercise I frequently give to students of fiction writing is to select a brief article in a newspaper or magazine: hard news or human interest, sports page or tabloid, what matters is that as you read it you are struck by a sense that within the words is a substance capable of expanding into a fictional universe.

In his wonderful essay "False Documents" novelist E. L. Doctorow writes that ". . . history shares with fiction a mode of mediating the world for the purpose of introducing meaning." He informs us that when the historian E. H. Carr characterized history not as a chronology, but as ". . . a continual process of interaction between the writer and the facts," he could as easily have been speaking of fiction, as well. This assignment proceeds from these fundamental qualities essential to all works of fiction.

Once the article is selected, the task is to interact with the thumbnail sketch of a narrative it contains: not as a journalist or historian would, but in a manner suggested by the job description Lionel Trilling gave to fiction writers in his essay on the Russian short-story writer Isaac Babel: ". . . to reveal the human fact within the veil of circumstances."

The object isn't to write an entire story, though that may come later.

The purpose of the exercise is to engage with the "facts" as freely and fully as possible, without worrying about the outcome or the shape of the entire narrative. It's not meant to be a laborious act—it should be an enjoyable process. It's enough to offer a significant glimpse at an imagined place derived from a real one, the people that inhabit it, and the unique conditions particular to their fate. It's also important to envision a point of view and to consider the persona of the voice that will guide the reader from the world of fact into the world you invent and discover.

Beginning with an idea that, at first, may not seem *yours* can liberate your imagination and affect your writer's process in new and unexpected ways.

— Adding more dimensional identity to strangers someone
   else has introduced us to can help us discover new ways of
   describing character.

— Considering the voice with which we will begin a story helps us pay more deliberate attention to the persona of the narrator—whether inside the story or not—and get a better understanding of how his/her sensibility can profoundly affect meaning.

— And finally (this especially applies to the larger narratives that can grow out of this exercise), by proceeding from a series of events we encounter rather than invent, we have an opportunity to conceive new ways of shaping a story. From the moment we perceive the fictional possibilities that reside in an article we are also foreseeing ways to organize and measure the story that can grow from the particular experience we are writing about, rather than from existing ideas of narrative structure.

This assignment, when done seriously, can not only offer students a new way to begin a story (one they may choose to finish: the next step would be to continue the story in the mode of dramatic presentation associated with conflict, and having the narrator step toward the back of the stage), it can strengthen their process in fundamental ways: understanding the necessity of trusting their writers' instincts, focusing on choice of subject matter; and in the ways specific to the craft of fiction I have spoken of above.

DEBRA SPARK

WEDDING CAKE
ASSIGNMENT

Debra Spark is the author of *Curious Attractions: Essays on Writing* and the novels *Coconuts for the Saint* and *The Ghost of Bridgetown*. She teaches at Colby College and lives with her husband and son in North Yarmouth, Maine.

For many years, the writer George Garrett taught in Charlottesville, Virginia. In the 1960s, a girl in a black raincoat (and pink high-top sneakers) regularly attended one of his classes. One day, though, she didn't appear. The subsequent week, a student read a poem titled "The Girl in the Black Raincoat." His fellow students were appalled. How could he—"he" was Henry Taylor, now a Pulitzer Prize–winning poet—write about someone from class? Someone they all knew? In turn, George Garrett was appalled.

Why did they suppose he couldn't write about her? Garrett assigned the *entire* class to write a poem or short story titled "The Girl in the Black Raincoat." A few writers in town tried it, too. Then, someone sent Garrett a piece for his anthology *The Girl in the Black Raincoat*. Garrett *wasn't* working on an anthology, but he thought, *Why not?* Now, if you scour used-book stores, you may find the resulting volume, published in 1966 and including work by Annie Dillard, Shelby Foote, Fred Chappell, and Mary Lee Settle, among others.

About fifteen years ago, National Public Radio's Susan Stamberg decided to repeat Garrett's experiment by asking him to select an image that she could assign to six different writers. Garrett picked "the wedding cake in the middle of the road," an image that appeals for being unlikely, but also for needing explanation. Though symbolically laden, the image requires facts (not abstractions) to understand.

I have a tape of the various writers who read their wedding cake story on air. One of the pleasures of listening—or of reading Susan Stamberg's 1992 anthology, *The Wedding Cake in the Middle of the Road: 23 Variations on a Theme*—is in comparing the responses, which range from the whimsical to the sourly dark.

For the longest time, *I* wanted to write a wedding-cake-in-the-middle-of-the-road story. But I couldn't come up with anything. I'd vaguely settled on a woman dressed as a wedding cake—I imagined the thick straps that would hold the wedding cake costume on her shoulders and how she would stop mid-road to say something to a companion. What an idiotic idea! Under what circumstances would a person be *dressed* as a wedding cake? A giant cell phone maybe. For promotional purposes. But a pastry? My lack of imagination annoyed me. Then one day, while working on my first novel, I realized, "Hey! I can get a cake in the middle of the road here!" The scene remains one of my favorite parts of my first novel.

Now when I teach, I ask students to come up with an interesting, somewhat puzzling image. They list their ideas on the blackboard then vote for a favorite, the image about which they'd most like to write.

In the fall of 2005, I taught at Deer Isle's Haystack Mountain School of Crafts. Though largely for those interested in textiles, ceramics, woodworking, jewelry, and the like, Haystack also offers the occasional writing class. I found my students particularly fun to work with. Given their visual background, they were already quite sensitive to the world around them.

So . . . I propose to *you* the exercise that the Haystack students created for one another.

EXERCISE

Write a short story using one of the following images:

1. The fish falling from the sky.

2. A lawn sign that reads, "Wife Wanted: Inquire Within."

A final note: the latter image is one hundred percent true. "I see that sign all the time when I drive from here to Bangor," said one woman in my class. Oh, the surprises of rural Maine!

A TABULA RASA EXPERIMENT

Katherine A. Vaz is a Briggs-Copeland Lecturer in Fiction at Harvard University. She's published two novels, *Saudade* and *Mariana*, which was selected by the U.S. Library of Congress as one of the Top 30 International Books of 1998. Her collection *Fado & Other Stories* won the 1997 Drue Heinz Literature Prize, and her short fiction has appeared in more than three dozen literary magazines. She is the first Portuguese-American to have her work recorded for the archives of the Hispanic Division of the Library of Congress.

M y students agree that the art of writing fiction presents not a time-management problem so much as a challenge of focus and attention. Maybe all of us are writing too much too swiftly. We tap into ideas, but we're not always creating the fictional realms that readers absolutely can't live without. We all know the difference between reading a book that's merely well done—engaging, even—and *falling inside a book,* a work we can't put down and that does nothing less than change the sound and color and meaning of the world. Some students of mine at Harvard mentioned a worry that their writing was too dredged in analysis: Their characters were busily, even wittily, observing everything at arm's length.

Here's one possible reason: There's often a fog at the front of our brains, a running list or inventory—what class work to do, which shoes to buy for a special event, whether we need to buy coffee.

How to clear that away, to get to the musicality and voice where originality is forged?

I've always taken counsel and solace from Simone Weil's and Franz Kafka's advice on the subject: Go into silence and *wait*. Don't grab the first word or idea that comes along. Wait for that sense of knowing you've plumbed down to the tough stuff, the difficult truth, the place where your characters tell you what's what or surprise you. Wait until you come up with the ways in which you feel incapable or lost or up against mystery, or, as the poet Fernando Pessoa says, you find yourself Always Astonished.

EXERCISE

Here's the experiment:

1. Spend an entire twenty-four hours (a whole weekend if you can) in "silence" and "waiting upon." Don't read, don't watch TV, don't flip through magazines. Don't clutter your brain. **Avoid busywork.** Some people are seized with a manic desire to clean their house, straighten files, or cook rather than be alone with their minds and hearts. Note what your impulse is to do, and return to a sense of calm and quiet and inaction. You don't have to take a vow of perfect silence or lie in a darkened room. Go ahead and chat with your roommate. Maybe listen to some music. Don't nap. This is wakefulness. Go for a walk or swim, but don't make this an excuse to run errands or go sightseeing or shopping.

2. Although you should refrain from plotting or writing, jot notes on what comes up for you. Images, memories, odd bits of speech, curious abstractions.

3. Some students said they "had too much to do" to undertake this. I told them to think of it as homework that would take them a day to complete.

The results may surprise you. Students notice that they back off and call it quits when they hit up against something that frightens them. In one case, it was as simple as a student not getting past the first hour because what welled up was her panic at not having a job set for after her graduation. But sometimes the images that occur are remarkable. One student said that he saw his friends with different faces on them, passing him in slow motion on the street. This leads to the next advice:

4. Free-associate what the images might mean. You might get a memory that surfaces: What's at the emotional root of it? Could that be where the source of some truth for you—a truth that can inform your fiction—lies? The student with the "friends with different faces" said that the image made no sense to him until we talked about it and he realized he had a mass of language and imagery trying to speak about betrayal.

Another student said she kept seeing birds in her mind's eye. She went for a walk and was startled to notice many flocks of birds. Months later, she realized that she'd been writing about her grandmother with hatred—accurately enough—but remembered that she had raised canaries, the one thing she'd done with compassion. This writer was able to enter the grandmother as a character with great fury and depth and empathy as a result. Oddly enough, too, when she presented this in class, a number of birds swooped and chattered at the window.

Some of you might remember when the space program did experiments to see how the mind would react to a lack of stimuli or isolation. They thought it would be a "clean slate" awaiting input, but what they discovered was that the musical patterns and dreamscapes that fuel desire, language, imagery, and the real truths we're trying to tap seem to rise up from within.

See what wells up: pictures and sounds, or notes dictating measures to you of a music that's purely your own.

One of Kafka's quotes: "Remain sitting at your table and listen. You need not even listen—simply wait. You need not even wait, just learn to become quiet, and still, and solitary. The world will freely offer itself to you to be unmasked. It has no choice; it will roll in ecstasy at your feet."

COLLAGE

Karen Brennan is the author of two collections of short stories, *The Garden in Which I Walk* and *Wild Desire* (winner of the Associated Writing Program Award). She is also the author of a memoir, *Being with Rachel*, and two collections of poems, *Here on Earth* and *The Real Enough World*. She is a professor at the University of Utah and a permanent faculty member at Warren Wilson's MFA Program for Writers.

EXERCISE

The following exercise works well for all genres of creative writing—fiction, poetry, memoir.

To make your collage you will use the following pieces:

1. a personal memory (or dream)

2. a current news story or cultural event

3. a detailed description of the natural world

Alternate these "pieces," paragraph by paragraph, until you assemble a story or poem or a text of creative nonfiction.

Do not worry how your pieces relate to one another; the longer you work on your collage, the more the pieces will begin to establish their own connections. At the beginning of your work, there will be a disjunctive feel which will smooth out as you go on with it.

It's best to write in block paragraphs. This way you will assist the reader in making sense of your collage. That is to say, you will signal to the reader that this is a collage piece and not a straightforward narrative with a plot trajectory. You may also choose to number your paragraphs or even title them.

For a more "postmodern" ambience, you may choose to keep your piece disjunctive, keep the pieces from relating too directly to one another.

For a slightly more traditional narrative, you may deliberately create transitions between pieces.

Make sure to alternate in order—this will help your reader to follow your text.

You're done when you "feel" done. This exercise demands surrendering to intuition. Leave your control-freak hat at home.

DAN WAKEFIELD

THE FIVE SENSES

Dan Wakefield is a novelist, journalist, and screenwriter. His books include *Returning: A Spiritual Journey, Releasing the Creative Spirit*, and *New York in the Fifties*.

This is an exercise that began as part of my workshops on "Spiritual Autobiography" and "Releasing the Creative Spirit," which have taken place in churches, synagogues, adult education centers, hospitals, health spas, universities, and prisons. Everyone has memories of all the sense experiences—taste, smell, touch, hearing, and sight, and those sense-memories never fail to evoke and elicit stories of our life experience. I use the exercises in some of my graduate writing workshops in the MFA program at Florida International University in Miami.

Aside from my own writing, which ranges from novels to memoirs, nothing has given me greater pleasure than leading people through these exercises based on the five senses. Every experience of someone else evokes a memory from your own life, one you have probably forgotten or buried way back in some hidden vault that is opened by simply hearing such phrases as "the taste of applesauce"; "the touch of corduroy"; "the smell of bacon frying"; "the sight of a sunset"; "the sound of rain." May they bring back your own meaningful memories and stories.

In my younger days I believed the common myth that creative inspiration—especially for writing—came from alcohol and drugs. When painful experience taught me otherwise, I looked for other ways to stimulate the creative imagination. I found a key in a definition of miracles by the great American writer Willa Cather in one of her novels. She wrote that "miracles . . . seem to me to rest not so much upon faces or voices or healing power coming from afar off, but from our own perception being made finer, so that for a moment our eyes can see, and our ears can hear what is there about us always."

EXERCISE

I realized that our five senses were doorways to evoke our own stories. I have tested this theory in writing classes and found it to be true—that using one of our natural senses that we take for granted—like taste, or smell, or hearing—can bring stories to our mind. To use this way of evocation through the sense of taste, for instance, you don't need to actually eat anything; you only have to think of the taste of something to bring forth stories. Once I simply suggested the taste of bacon to a group of factory workers, and one of them wrote and read to the group a moving story that was evoked for him. The heart of the story was that as a child, when he woke up and smelled bacon frying he knew it would be a good day in his home; if he woke and didn't smell the bacon, it meant his parents had hangovers from drinking too much the night before, and things in his house that day would not be pleasant.

Here is a list of common foods that may trigger a memory or scene in your mind:

The taste of applesauce; the taste of popcorn; the taste of coffee; the taste of chocolate; the taste of hot dogs.

Whichever taste brings something to mind, write everything you remember about it for the next ten minutes. Write the way you would tell a friend about what you remember. Don't edit or second-guess yourself, just let the story come forth. The story is in the taste.

BIRTH OF A STORY IN AN HOUR OR LESS

Crystal Wilkinson teaches creative writing and literature in the MFA in Creative Writing Program at Indiana University in Bloomington. She is the author of *Water Street*, which was a finalist for both the Orange Prize and the Hurston/Wright Legacy Award in Fiction, and *Blackberries, Blackberries*. Her writing also received the 2002 Chaffin Award for Appalachian Literature and has appeared in various literary journals and anthologies, including *Southern Exposure*; *LIT*; *Obsidian II*; the *Indiana Review*; *Gumbo: Stories by Black Writers*; *Confronting Appalachian Stereotypes*; *Home and Beyond: A Half-Century of Short Stories by Kentucky Writers*; and *Gifts from Our Grandmothers*.

Inventing a fiction is like giving birth. It is about the act of creating a living, breathing character and placing him or her in a realistic situation. As fiction writers we take everything we know about how the world works and bridge it to another level of understanding. When we invent a character we inhabit someone else's voice, body and mind. This act of explaining the movements, the actions, the psychological history of someone we don't fully understand is precisely the art of fiction.

This exercise is intended to be done in several parts and may take up to an hour to complete. It could also be divided up into several days.

EXERCISE

Part I: The Voice

At birth our first modes of communication are oral, so let's begin there.

Imagine two characters having a conversation. Maybe they are talking about a third person. Perhaps one of them has a problem. Write only dialogue. Focus only on inventing a conversation.

Example:

A: I'm not feeling well today.

B: Really, what's wrong?

A: I've got a headache.

B: Did I tell you what Bob said last night?

Keep writing until you have two full pages of dialogue.

Part II: Your Characters' Place in the World

Imagine where this conversation is taking place. Describe the place, filling in as many details as you can just taking in the area. What objects are there? Are there any sensory details you've missed? Weather? Are there smells? Sounds?

Part III: Who Are You?

Choose one of these characters to focus on and answer the following questions. Each answer puts you closer to knowing this person you've invented. Try not to overthink your answers; just move as quickly as you can down the list, not stopping to judge. Answer honestly in the moment.

1. Describe your character physically, from head to toe.

2. What relationships are important to your character? Why?

3. What does your character do? Profession? Pleasure?

4. What is your character most afraid of?

5. What does your character want?

You may also add to this list.

Part IV: Making a Scene

Isn't that just like a baby? You've put your time and effort into giving it birth and now it wants to act out, make a scene. But that is precisely what we want our characters to do, to act. Fiction is made of actions and reactions.

Now it's time to put all that you have discovered to work. Write three separate scenes that may occur at different points in your story. The scenes will not necessarily be chronological. Try to write at least one to two pages for each scene. Make sure your scenes open, close and something takes place. The "something" is up to you.

A brief definition of a scene: A scene gives the illusion of real life in fiction. It slows things down to real time and allows a reader to see something happen. A scene most often includes dialogue and should include some combination of the things you've done above: description of the setting, a character's feelings and thoughts, gestures, action and observations from the narrator or author. A scene occurs in one place.

Scene 1—Before the Conversation

Imagine a time in your character's(s') life before the conversation or before their problem. This could be immediately before they began the conversation with the other character(s) or long before, even to childhood. But it must be **before** the conversation. Go for it.

Try to include all you know about these characters so far. In thinking about their past even (if you choose to write from that place) what may have contributed to the problem they are experiencing now at the time of your story's invention.

Scene 2—During the Conversation

Write a scene that occurs during the conversation. You will most likely rely heavily on your dialogue section here. Include the description of the setting; include any objects in the room that your character(s) may come in contact with. What gestures are they using? Do they have an accent? Are there interruptions? By whom? By what? Does your character's mind wander during the conversation? What is he/she thinking about?

Scene 3—After the Conversation

This scene occurs after the conversation. Include as many elements of scene as you think necessary but allow one of the following to occur:

1. Your character's problem is solved.

2. Your character(s) decide that this problem is going to be with them for a while and so they must learn to deal with it.

For this scene think toward change, think toward some closure at this moment in your character's life.

Purpose

If you think of a story as having a beginning, middle, and an end, what you have in these three scenes could mimic the structure of a story. At this point you should have a skeleton of sorts in front of you, at least three pages toward a story that you can build on. In your process you may have discovered that the story needs to begin with one of these three scenes or someplace else altogether. The objective here is to cover a lot of ground toward the invention of a story in a small amount of time. This exercise forces you to make some decisions that may address multiple possibilities for a single story idea. It is an interesting way of jumping into a story quickly instead of forming your decisions in a chronological or even logical way. It gets you out of thinker-pose and gets you writing.

SURREALISM EXERCISE, OR THINKING OUTSIDE THE BOX

Laurie Foos is the author of the novels *Ex Utero, Portrait of the Walrus by a Young Artist, Twinship, Bingo Under the Crucifix*, and *Before Elvis There Was Nothing*. She teaches in the low-residency MFA program at Lesley University, in Cambridge, Massachusetts, and lives on Long Island with her husband and daughter.

It is my belief that there are two components necessary to any writer's growth. The first is the writer's ability to access his/her unconscious, and the second is the writer's willingness to take risks. Each writer has his/her own tastes and proclivities, naturally, and may or may not have a fondness or a desire to delve into surrealism. What's important about this exercise is that, in general, it allows the writer to "think outside the box," to move into territory with which he/she might not be familiar or comfortable.

As a writer, I stress with my students the necessity of moving out of one's comfort zone, to try new things. Risk taking allows us to grow as writers. It's also important to have some fun now and again, which is another of my credos, and this exercise is designed to be fun.

This exercise is designed to open the parameters of what we know as realistic fiction by causing the writer to stretch those limits from the first line. The ideas behind the exercise come mostly from Kafka's *Metamorphosis* and the famous first line, "Gregor Samsa awoke from uneasy dreams to find himself transformed into a gigantic insect."

The exercise can be done in a group setting with partners, or it can be done alone. If you are doing the exercise alone, be sure to do the exercise as written, and take care not to cheat and read ahead. You may even want to cover up Step Two with a piece of paper or with your hand.

The idea of the exercise is to begin your story *in media res* and to enter territory you may not have entered before. To give too much thought to where you are going would negate the governing ideas behind surrealistic fiction, and that is that it should allow for the workings of the unconscious to be its guide.

EXERCISE

Step One

If you're doing this exercise in a group, have the person on your right (or left, whichever you prefer) write down three words. It's important that the words be written down *quickly,* with no thought as to where they might be going:

Any -ing verb

A body part

An inanimate object

(If you're doing the exercise alone, write the words down *as quickly as possible*—and again, don't read ahead!)

Step Two

Insert the words into the following prompt:

After a long day of *-ing verb*, he/she discovered that his/her *body part* had grown a/an *inanimate object*.

Begin!

OVERCOMING DRY SPELLS

Leslie Schwartz is the author of the *Los Angeles Times* best-selling novel *Angels Crest*, which has been translated into nine languages. Her first novel, *Jumping the Green*, won the James Jones Literary Society Award for Best First Novel. She has had numerous short-story publications, and her nonfiction has appeared in many newspapers and magazines throughout the United States. She was chosen as *Kalliope* magazine's Woman Writer of the Year for 2004. She teaches writing at the UCLA Extension Writers' Program and at the Iowa Summer Writing Festival at the University of Iowa. She is also the literary reporter for the Council of Literary Magazines and Presses in New York City. She is currently the program director for PEN USA's Emerging Voices program and is on the board of directors for PEN USA.

I have never much believed in writer's block. Just the term itself is insidious. Any time we label something, it becomes real, and it's not as if we writers need any more neuroses than we already have! Yet, there *are* times in my own work when I just can't seem to muster the energy to write. Or the words don't come. Or they come, but as if through a swamp of doubts and misgivings. This doesn't happen often, but when it does, I usually take that as a signal that it's time to rest.

I remember a couple of days after my second novel hit bookstores, I looked at the novel I was working on and thought to myself, "I can't do this." Some combination of the fear of publishing and the strange letdown that comes with it, combined with my doubt about the personal authenticity of the story I was struggling with, made me want to give up writing altogether. That day, as I sat there staring at the blank screen, my agent happened to call, and I told him how awful I was feeling about the new novel I was writing. He told me to take the day off. "Take your daughter to the beach," he said, "and get back to it another day."

It was the best advice anyone could have given me, and taking it made all the difference in the world.

Sometimes the only cure for those writer's blues, is to give in to them. Shut the computer off, go to a movie, forget about it. But other times, this can be absolutely the wrong thing to do. It's up to you to know the difference between making up excuses not to write and taking a much-needed reprieve for a day or two.

EXERCISE

Here are a few of my favorite exercises to jump-start a flagging writing session:

- Write about what you *would* write about if you weren't stuck.

- Take one or two of your characters and put them in a stuck elevator with:

  → Your mother

  → The devil

  → God

  → Yourself . . . and let the action roll without censure.

- Before you sit down to write, take a long walk alone in a quiet place and envision the next scene of your story. Don't ever come to the computer empty-headed. Don't ever call up your story without first knowing where you want to take it next.

· Break the writing down into small pieces. E. L. Doctorow said, "Writing a novel is like driving a car at night. You only have to see as far as your headlights, but you can make the whole trip that way." Don't fret about the end. Don't even fret about the next scene. All books are written one word at a time.

· Deadlines work for some people; for others they don't. If you are someone who works well under deadlines, set them, but remember to make them reasonable. There is nothing more counterproductive and depressing than not meeting your deadlines. I set myself time deadlines, rather than page-length deadlines. Each day I allot myself a certain amount of time to write, given the rest of my schedule that day. Sometimes it's a half hour, sometimes it's three hours, but whatever it is, I stick to it. It's a way to meet a goal without having to worry how many pages I've written.

· Put together a writing group of trusted writers who are adept at giving strong, critical feedback and support. Sometimes just talking to another writer about the difficulties helps.

· And finally, keep your writing in perspective. Don't take it all so seriously. One of the biggest breakthroughs I had was the day I realized I wasn't going to change the world with my work, that it was only myself for whom I was writing, and perhaps only myself who would be moved or affected by the process of creating story. Once I realized that, I saw how silly it was to attach so much importance to the process. Remember, writing is hard work, but it should be fun too!

VIRGIL SUÁREZ

FIELD TRIP

Virgil Suárez is the author of, most recently, *90 Miles: Selected and New Poems*. He teaches at Bennington College's low-residency MFA as well as in the creative-writing program at Florida State University where he is a full professor. He is the author of four novels, two memoirs, two collections of stories, and eight poetry collections, including *Banyan, Palm Crows, Guide to the Blue Tongue*, as well as the editor of eight anthologies. He lives in the great city of Miami, which he loves and which has a great many gorgeous cemeteries.

This exercise, though similar to what I would call "fish out of water" or as Diane Thiel calls it in her book *Open Roads* "Innocent Perspective," I think of as a Field Trip exercise where the objective is to travel to a place, not too far, that will make an emotional impact on you, the writer.

I think some of the best work I've produced comes from having explored such never-been-there territory. I feel this way about going to hospitals, attorneys' offices, mechanics, and certainly a morgue or cemetery. "Field Trip" is such an excursion. The idea is to go to a place that is going to draw certain high levels of emotion from you. I think of the cemetery as being such a place. Every semester I take my undergraduate poetry workshop to the local cemetery here in Tallahassee, which is right next to campus and which has lots of fairly old (and famous) folks buried there.

Why? Because it is a nice way to talk and write about mortality, about those issues that are relevant always, and is also a great way to talk about some of the Romantics and writers like Edgar Allan Poe.

EXERCISE

The exercise, though some students think it a bit morbid, is to write about Death, something relating to death and dying, to what it must feel like. Oftentimes, I ask the students to write a letter from the Great Beyond; to focus on the passing of time, anything to work toward voice. I'm always pleased that of all the things the students mention, they mention the "Field Trip" assignment.

The exercise has many possibilities including writing in genres, writing from the reality of being in a place and seeing it. The level of emotion comes from perhaps a few voices that begin to speak. It has high impact on the heart over the intellect. Usually it begins in dread and fear and moves toward a certain level of clarity via memory. Memory, then, becomes the catalyst for voice.

We learn that we often don't have to travel far to produce interesting work, but often, when we yearn for something new, a breakthrough of sorts, we can take a walk through a cemetery, commune with our feelings of time's passage.

Not much is required of the writer, other than perceptibility and access to lots of silence, and a cemetery offers all the silence the heart can withstand.

DAVID MICHAEL KAPLAN

SMUSHING SEED IDEAS TOGETHER

David Michael Kaplan is the author of *Comfort*, a collection of short stories, *Skating in the Dark*, a novel, and *Revision: A Creative Approach to Writing and Rewriting Fiction*. His short stories have appeared in *The Atlantic Monthly, Playboy, Redbook, TriQuarterly, Doubletake, ACM, StoryQuarterly*, and many other literary magazines, and have been anthologized in *The Best American Short Stories, The O. Henry Prize Stories*, and *The Scribner Anthology of Contemporary Short Fiction*, among others. He is the 1999 winner of the Nelson Algren Short Story Award. He teaches fiction writing at Loyola University in Chicago.

Short stories—and novels—start from what I call a "seed idea." It's an image, idea, or experience, however small, which gets your imaginative juices going enough to make you want to develop it into a more fully fleshed-out *story* idea. For Faulkner, seeing a little girl's muddy underpants while she was on a swing was the seed idea for *The Sound and the Fury*; for you, it might be overhearing someone on a bus, saying that his girlfriend broke his glasses in a fight the previous night, or seeing a picture in a magazine of a rider on horseback, trudging through a heavy winter snow. You mull over the seed idea: Who is this rider? Where's he going? Where's he come from? What's happened to him? What's going to happen? Who else is in his world, and in this story?

You make notes, imagine characters, and sketch out possible scenes, as you try to develop the seed idea into a story idea which is original, exciting, and emotionally powerful.

This is an exercise which illustrates a technique to help you get to that story.

EXERCISE

First, select three "seed ideas"—things you've overheard, seen, been told, have happened to you, whatever—which you feel could be the starting point for a character or a conflict in a story. These should be *brief*—a phrase or a sentence is often enough—and *specific* and *concrete*, not vague and abstract. Not, "a man is in a moral quandary," or "a woman pines for a lost love." Hard to get imaginatively involved with either of those. More something like:

An old man sits rocking and talking to himself on the El . . .

A little boy sees someone stealing a dollar bill from the collection plate as it's being passed around . . .

A woman on a cell phone says, "There's nothing anyone can do now. It's over, done with. I'm leaving town tonight. . . ."

Got your three? All pretty different, aren't they?

Now take the one that interests you the most, and spend fifteen or so minutes developing it, in sketch/notes form, into a story idea. As far as you can take it in fifteen minutes. At the very least, try to indicate who the main character or characters are, where and when it's taking place, what the conflict(s) might be, and maybe a bit of what happens. Don't worry about "writing good"—just make notes. Remember—you're not writing the story, just sketching it out, however far you get in fifteen minutes.

Now take *one* of the remaining two seed ideas and combine it with the story idea you've been developing. "Smush" it in, as it were, and try to make the two work together. To do this, both the original seed idea, and/or the second seed idea, and/or the developing story idea may change: it's the rare second seed idea which neatly and conveniently plops into the original story idea you've been sketching. That's okay, because these changes often lead you to a revised story idea which is more interesting than the one you were first working on. Again, spend about fifteen minutes sketching out this revised story.

For example—using one of the seed ideas above—you may have first been developing a story about a little boy seeing a man stealing from a collection plate. Now you try to smush that together with the second unrelated seed idea of a woman desperately saying on her phone that she has to leave town. To make them work together, you might change the story into one in which a woman who has been embezzling petty cash from her company fears she's been caught and is about to be confronted. She's desperately trying to figure out what to do, and at one point calls a friend to confess what she's done and that she doesn't see any way out but to run away . . . and so on. The little boy has been dropped, the man stealing from the plate has been transformed into a woman embezzler. And so a new story idea develops as a result of this smushing together of two different seed ideas—often a story which is more original and more exciting than the first one.

Now, take another fifteen minutes and try to smush the third seed idea in too. It may or may not work, but try. Again, things may change. Continuing our example, you may suddenly see that the old man rocking on the El seed idea could be transformed into your woman embezzler—and could suggest a final scene in the story, in which she in despair, everything closing in around her, winds up not running away, but staying on the El, rocking, unable to move.

A basic aspect of creativity is the yoking together of the seemingly disparate, of seeing connections and possibilities where there seemed to be none. Geniuses may make these connections unconsciously; we who aren't geniuses might need to "jump-start" this process. This is one way to do it, not only for this exercise, but whenever we're working on story ideas. You don't have to limit yourself to a few minutes and three seed ideas, after all. (If you faithfully record your seed ideas, as they come to you, in a journal or notebook, you'll soon have a treasure trove to work with.) Try smushing different ones into any story you're developing. Take as much time as you need. Some won't work, of course. But some will. Guaranteed. And guaranteed to lead you to some original and amazing story ideas.

THE WRITING EXERCISE: A RECIPE

Kathleen Spivack is the author of six books of poetry: *The Break-Up Variations, The Beds We Lie In* (nominated for a Pulitzer Prize), *The Honeymoon, Swimmer in the Spreading Dawn, The Jane Poems*, and *Flying Inland*. She is also the author of a novel, *Unspeakable Things*, and a memoir, *Robert Lowell, A Personal Memoir*. Her most recent work can be seen in *The Massachusetts Review* and *The Virginia Quarterly Review*, among others. Other publications include *The New Yorker, Ploughshares, The Atlantic Monthly, Poetry, The Paris Review, The Kenyon Review, Agni*, and *New Letters*. She has taught in France full- or half-time since 1990. Ms. Spivack has held posts as Visiting Professor at the University of Paris VII–VIII, the University of Tours, the University of Versailles, and at the Ecole Supérieure Polytechnique. She was also a Fulbright Professor in Creative Writing, France (1993–94). She has received grants from the National Endowment for the Arts, the Massachusetts Artists Foundation, the Bunting Institute, the Howard Foundation, and the Massachusetts Council for the Arts and Humanities. In Boston and Paris Kathleen Spivack directs the Advanced Writing Workshop, an intensive program for professional writers.

INGREDIENTS AND PREPARATION

Before bedtime, pick up the alarm clock. Set it to ring two hours earlier than your usual wake-up time.

Sleep. Or don't. But get up anyway.

Put a mug of coffee, tea, or other comfort in your hands. Now go to your desk immediately. Sit down. Look dazed. Open the computer-mind.

Work on a writing project—somehow—for two hours. Don't complain.

Part One

Do this for two weeks, steadily. Your body may react with fever, aches, and a sense of dullness. Ignore this. It is to be expected.

Part Two

Do this for two months. Do it for a year. Increase the amount of time spent with your dominatrix. Obey her. Pain, delusions of grandeur and self-doubt are typical symptoms. Continue. The virus is beginning to take hold.

Part Three

Congratulations. You are now satisfactorily infected. Write! Do this for the rest of your life.

POINT OF VIEW

A STORY TO TELL

Nina de Gramont is the fiction editor of the literary magazine *Ecotone* and the author of a collection of short stories, *Of Cats and Men*. Her fiction has appeared in a variety of magazines including *Nerve*, *Post Road*, *The Exquisite Corpse*, *The Cream City Review*, and *Seventeen*. She teaches creative writing and composition at the University of North Carolina, Wilmington, and lives in Wrightsville Beach.

Everybody has one. I'm not talking about epic adventures or grand escapades. I'm talking about anecdotes: the personal stories we relay in order to give people an idea of who we are. It could be a story from your childhood, something you don't remember yourself but that you've heard your mother tell a thousand times. It could be something silly or triumphant that you did in college, or something fantastic and barely believable that happened to you and your best friend from high school. If you have more than one of these stories, chances are the people closest to you know them all.

My husband has one from his college days about fracturing his skull: to impress a girl, he tried to swing down from a third-story window using the branch of a tree (Errol Flynn style, as he always says). I've heard him tell this story so many times that I could easily recite it verbatim, employing his tone and inflections.

These are the stories we tell early in a relationship: when we first meet a friend or a love interest, and want to convey not only a sense of our personal history, but of ourselves.

A first-person narrative needs to do more than just fill the reader in on the action. It needs to be multidimensional—illuminating a character not only through the information she gives willingly, but the accidental information she gives through preoccupation and perspective. A writer needs to create a voice that characterizes this narrator in a way she might not be able to characterize herself, at least not directly.

EXERCISE

Think of an anecdote you habitually tell when you first come to know someone—a piece of history that's sad, strange, or funny. Make sure it's the one you've already told everyone who knows you well, the one you've told a thousand times.

Now put it down on paper. Try to capture—exactly—the way you tell it: the words that you stress, and the phrases that you use. It should read like a transcript of your own voice.

When you read what you've written, look for clues to your own personality. Pay attention to what the anecdote says about your sense of humor, your personal obsessions, your core character.

Next, ascribe the anecdote to one of your own fictional characters. Imagine the same event occurring to her, and think about how this person might perceive and experience it. Write another first-person narrative about this experience, this time in the voice of your fictional character.

FIRST-PERSON POINT OF VIEW: IMAGINING AND INHABITING CHARACTER

Maureen McCoy is the author of four novels, *Junebug, Divining Blood, Summertime,* and *Walking After Midnight,* which was noted in *Book Lust*'s Elvis chapter. She is a professor of English at Cornell University and also lives in Taos, New Mexico. Recent short fiction, "How Tiny Tim Entered the Witness Protection Program," was published in *Epoch*; "Snakers" appeared in the anthology *Photographers, Writers, and the American Scene: Visions of Passage.*

Writing in first person comes naturally to many writing students, but because the narrator is often barely a smidgen removed from the writer, the writer risks missing opportunities for character development in a fresh voice. Also, the writer's wholesale identification with the narrator may obstruct character development of others in the story. To go more deeply into the imagined, and into the craft of character revelation, I use the following first-person point-of-view exercise.

EXERCISE

Recall a conflict, however slight, and certainly not of life-or-death magnitude, with a person who is older and who was in opposition to your needs or desires. You may want to use an argument with a parent: about a chore, a tattoo appointment, or a carelessly conceived plan to climb Kilimanjaro. Or, perhaps you'll recall a prickly incident with a stranger. Example: a bus driver who demanded that you leave your expensive latte on the curb. Conjure up and scribble down all that you can of the emotions and sensory experience from that time. Get whipped into a lather of righteousness, confusion, hope, irritation, etc., all over again.

Now write a version of this conflict as a first-person account from the point of view of the other character in the story. You will have a good start on a deeply imagined story or monologue, with character at the heart, and motivation revealed. Draw on aspects of character such as quirks of grammar and diction, the character's past experience, personal hopes or fears or dreams, all that might tumble forth with vivid urgency once you shift that "I." You will create a character from the inside out who is vivid because you have fully, if briefly, inhabited that character.

CLYDE EDGERTON

YOU-ME-I-YOU IN THE CAFETERIA

Clyde Edgerton is the author of eight novels: *Raney* (translated into Japanese), *Walking Across Egypt*, *The Floatplane Notebooks* (translated into German), *Killer Diller*, *In Memory of Junior*, *Redeye*, *Where Trouble Sleeps*, and *Lunch at the Piccadilly*. His newest book, *Solo: My Adventures in the Air*, is nonfiction. He is the recipient of a Guggenheim Fellowship, a Lyndhurst Fellowship, the North Carolina Award for Literature, a Distinguished Alumni Award from the University of North Carolina–Chapel Hill Education Department, and five Notable Book Awards from *The New York Times*. He teaches creative writing in the MFA program at the University of North Carolina, Wilmington.

Point of view is, in *my* view, the most interesting and sometimes frustrating "element" of fiction. Before I knew what I was doing as a fiction writer, dealing with point of view was pretty easy, but as I learned more about point of view my thinking on the subject seemed to become denser.

One thing is certain: your writing about another character's emotions and thoughts depends on the magic trick of getting into his/her head. Additionally, as fiction writers we need to write not only about our best selves, but also our worst selves.

EXERCISE

Here's an exercise, moving from nonfiction into fiction, that allows practice with two points of view:

1. Of the people you know well—or fairly well—and dislike most, pick one.

2. Imagine that you walk into a cafeteria for lunch. There are a few people sitting here and there. Over in the corner, sitting alone and reading the newspaper, is the person you dislike. Write a first-person account of what you're thinking as you get your food and find a seat. Write about a half page.

3. Now get out a clean sheet of paper and imagine that you are the person you dislike. Get into that person's head as he/she sees you coming into the cafeteria. Write about a half page.

4. Discuss with others your experience in writing this exercise. What was easy about it? Difficult? Why?

MARTHA COOLEY

GETTING CHARACTERS' AGES RIGHT

Martha Cooley is the author of two novels, *The Archivist* (which has been published in over ten foreign markets) and *Thirty-three Swoons* (also in translation in Italian). Her short fiction and essays have appeared in *AGNI* and *Washington Square*, among other venues. She is an assistant professor of English at Adelphi University in Garden City, New York, and a member of the core faculty of the Bennington Writing Seminars at Bennington College in Vermont. She has also taught in the MA program in writing at Boston University.

Fiction-writing students often struggle to solve two common challenges involving age: one, how to let the reader know what the ages of characters are without necessarily stating or signaling those ages outright, and two, how to ensure that the characters' ages (whether implicitly or explicitly signaled) are in fact credible—that is, made believable by virtue of appropriate and effective physical, emotional, psychological, and behavioral *details,* and/or by a speaking or narrating *voice* (in a first-person narration) that feels right for that character at that age.

One of the most typical pitfalls is getting the ages of children right. A good story writer can, of course, make any child-character— even one with traits that would normally be deemed unusual for his or her age—credible within the terms of the writer's particular story-world. The trick is to make sure that all signals point in the same direction, as it were, so the reader accepts without question that particular child-character's age, or has no difficulty concluding what that age is—and, too, so the age remains credible throughout the telling of the story.

A four-year-old who comes up with complex and highly successful schemes for humiliating her ten-year-old brother? Maybe, but only in a story in which we can accept that this girl is decidedly precocious. An eighth-grade, urban-dwelling boy who shows no interest whatsoever in money? Unlikely, unless he's been raised by parents who have shielded him utterly from the outside world. A teenager whose snack foods are milk and graham crackers? Yes, perhaps—if that's how the kid has been raised, and if we believe that s/he has little interest in or capacity for breaking a childhood habit. But no, if the kid normally hangs out with McDonald's-munching peers whom, we sense, would surely notice and comment on such aberrant eating choices. (Unless, of course, those choices are an act of defiance, and/or the kid *enjoys* getting ribbed ...) Invariably, the challenge is to fit any and all signals about characters' ages to the story at hand—so there's no point at which the reader will think, *wait a minute, isn't this kid* ten, *not five? Or, how old* is *this kid, anyway? Or, why should I believe that* this *bright teenager is talking in* that *dopey voice?*

EXERCISE

Two siblings, a six-year-old girl and her thirteen-year-old sister, are walking to school. (The older sister drops the younger one off at her first-grade classroom each morning, before heading to her own eighth-grade homeroom.) A woman they've never seen approaches them and asks for money, then threatens to tell the principal "what she knows about them."

Continuing from this setup, write a scene from a third-person-omniscient viewpoint (i.e., favoring no character in particular but rather giving all three equal play). In this scene, do not identify the girls' or the stranger's ages outright; allow the reader to deduce them. Have the girls speak first in response to the stranger and then (after she departs) with each other. In addition to speech, include details of all three characters' dress and physical gestures.

Now rewrite the scene from a first-person point of view, choosing the six-year-old as the narrator. Then do the same from the older sister's viewpoint.

Throughout the exercise, pay attention to several basic questions this scene must address: Are these characters' behaviors and speech pegged appropriately to their ages? Are they consonant with the action, tone, and diction of the narrative as a whole? Do we believe each one is the age that she is?

WHAT ARE THEY THINKING? A POINT-OF-VIEW EXERCISE

Paula Morris is the author of two novels, *Queen of Beauty* and *Hibiscus Coast*, both published by Penguin Books in her native New Zealand. She teaches creative writing at Tulane University in New Orleans.

EXERCISE

This three-part exercise explores choosing a point of view—an act that David Lodge, in *The Art of Fiction*, calls "arguably the most important single decision a novelist has to make."

Find a photograph from a magazine, newspaper, or book that includes at least two people. The photograph can be historical or contemporary; it may be a posed group shot in a photographer's studio, a picture taken during a war or major event, or a photo of a crowded market in a faraway location. (Travel magazines and *National Geographic* are very useful here.)

Once you have selected a photograph, write three short paragraphs describing the scene—one from the point of view of one person in the photograph, one from the point of view of a second person in the photograph, and one from a third person not included in the picture. This third person could be the photographer, an onlooker, or someone leaving the scene; it could be a person who knows the people in the picture, or has nothing to do with them at all.

Write in the third person. In each paragraph, focus on what each person is seeing and feeling, the way he or she perceives the place, the occasion, the other people in the picture. Don't forget things like the weather, or the time of day or year—everything that contributes to the way a person responds to a scene. Think about how each character feels about the place and the other people, if she is in love with another person in the picture, if he hates being caught in the rain, if she is worrying about something else in her life.

There are numerous variations to this exercise. Students can write the whole exercise in the first person, or a mixture of third and first. They can write one scene description in the first person, one in the second person, and one in the third person, exploring the way manipulating point of view affects the tone and psychic distance in fiction. Students can also work in pairs, each describing the scene in the photograph from a different character's point of view: the resulting synergies or differences reveal the idiosyncrasies of a particular point of view.

For this exercise, I've accumulated a number of vintage postcards and narrative pictures from magazines. Sometimes I ask students to choose a picture, and sometimes I simply hand the pictures out. I ask some groups of students to bring family photographs from home—preferably of relatives they don't know very well, like great-grandparents—which they can use themselves or swap with a neighbor.

Asking students to make the imaginative leap into more than one character, both within and outside the picture, helps them to see the possibilities and limitations in the choice of point of view. It also helps them understand the way a point of view dictates the way the setting, characters, action, and emotional currents of a scene are presented.

DAPHNE KALOTAY

THIRD-PERSON NARRATION AND "PSYCHIC DISTANCE"

Daphne Kalotay is the author of the fiction collection *Calamity and Other Stories*, which includes work from *Michigan Quarterly Review, The Missouri Review, Good Housekeeping, AGNI, The Literary Review,* and *Prairie Schooner.* She is a graduate of Boston University's Creative Writing Program and has taught literature and creative writing at Middlebury College in Vermont and Boston University. Kalotay lives in Brookline, Massachusetts.

This is an exercise that I reserve for my upper-level classes, because it involves nuanced reading and extreme attention to details of language. It reflects my own continued interest in the very specific techniques that are available to us as writers and the decisions we are always making, whether consciously or subconsciously, as we set out to put our narratives on paper.

When I teach, my goal is to make sure that my intermediate and advanced students take the time to make more deliberate decisions about basic elements such as narration, with a real understanding of the advantages and limits of first-, second- or third-person perspective. What I like about this exercise, which has its origins in John Gardner's definition of "psychic distance," is that it allows me to spend time discussing the many flexibilities that the third person allows in terms of emotional intensity.

I myself when I write am often more comfortable in the third person, and I notice that many writers I love and reread (Chekhov and Tolstoy, Bowen and Stafford, Gallant and Trevor) are particularly adept at making the most of the third-person point of view. I have my students write three versions (same scene and characters) of varying distance and am always thrilled when they realize how infinitely broad the possibilities are in terms of the many ways to tell a single story.

EXERCISE

Students often assume that the best way to create a sense of closeness to a protagonist is to write in the first person. At the same time, when they write in the third person they often ignore the many available ways to vary the reader's closeness to (or distance from) the protagonist and all that happens to him/her. The following exercise explores this crucial aspect, which John Gardner, in *The Art of Fiction*, called **psychic distance**.

Gardner defines psychic distance as "the distance the reader feels between himself and the events in the story." He gives the following examples of how variations in third-person narration create this sense of distance or closeness:

1. It was winter of the year 1853. A large man stepped out of a doorway.

2. Henry J. Warburton had never much cared for snowstorms.

3. Henry hated snowstorms.

4. God, how he hated these damn snowstorms.

Take a moment to examine the elements that manipulate distance in each of these sentences. In the first example, we see the nameless man from afar and are not privy to any of his thoughts or emotions; the traditional structure of that first sentence maintains a certain reserve. In the second example we are close enough for more colloquial diction ("had never much cared for") and to hear the character's feelings about snow, but the man is introduced to us in a formal way, by his full name. In the third example we are already on a first-name basis, which takes us even closer, and we hear his feelings about snow in a less delicate manner. By the fourth example we're practically in his head, hear his own language, are so close to him that we don't need to be told his name—and there's no need for restraint in the way he expresses himself.

Now, take a look at some works you admire that are written in the third person, and examine the use of formal or informal diction, traditional versus colloquial sentence structure, thought versus action, etc.; note how such techniques are already at work in the very opening sentence. Some great examples of carefully maintained tonal distance—despite closeness of thought—can be found in Flannery O'Connor's stories ("The grandmother didn't want to go to Florida. . . .") just as wonderful examples of closeness can be found in Virginia Woolf (see the opening paragraph of *Mrs. Dalloway*). Notice how writers orchestrate shifts in distance, as in the opening of Fitzgerald's "Bernice Bobs Her Hair," which begins at a far-away angle and then zooms in, like a camera lens, to bring us face-to-face with the character.

Now look back at your own work in progress. Rewrite the opening paragraph to your story three times, each in the third person, each at a different level of psychic distance. Try one that is so close, the very vocabulary is that of the character. Try one so far off, it's as if we're watching from a helicopter flying slowly overhead. Finally, try the most difficult of all: something in between. (Perhaps we know what the characters are thinking, but the diction is formal enough to keep us slightly at bay—or vice versa.)

Being able to control shifts in psychic distance—maintaining a particular level of closeness—is one of the most useful techniques at our disposal. It's also a real challenge and takes a lot of practice. I encourage you to experiment with the way the entire feel of a story can change when you manipulate language and narration. Try rewriting the opening paragraph of an existing, published story from a different degree of distance and see how different it sounds. Be aware of the power of this important tool—and have fun with it as you create your own stories.

LOOK BACKWARD, ANGEL

Eileen Pollack is the author of a novel, *Paradise, New York*; a collection of short fiction, *The Rabbi in the Attic and Other Stories*; and a work of creative nonfiction, *Woman Walking Ahead: In Search of Catherine Weldon and Sitting Bull*. She is an associate professor on the MFA faculty at the University of Michigan.

My favorite point of view is first-person retrospective, in which a first-person narrator looks back on an event that occurred a long time ago, or at least far enough in the past to allow the narrator to gain new perspective. This is a particularly useful point of view for narrating an event that happened to a child, since it allows the narrator to alternate between the vocabulary and insights of an adult and the more limited language, thoughts, and feelings of a child. To see how a master handles this p.o.v., you might want to look at novels such as *To Kill a Mockingbird* by Harper Lee or *So Long, See You Tomorrow* by William Maxwell or various first-person stories by Alice Munro, Raymond Carver, Richard Ford, etc.

EXERCISE

Think of the most immoral thing you've ever done. Narrate the event in the first person ("I"), in the present tense. Try to re-create for your readers a sense of what it was like to commit that offense, to experience those events. Re-create the setting, the various characters involved, who said what to whom, who did what and when, your role in these events, what you did, said, thought and felt.

Use the language you would have used at the time. (Note: if you've never done anything immoral, think of something you almost did that was immoral and pretend you actually did it. If you've never even come close to doing something immoral, think of something immoral that someone else did, preferably someone you know, pretend you're that person and write the story in first person, present tense, as if you were the person carrying out the immoral act.)

Now, think back on that event in a new way, as someone older with a new perspective. (If the event happened at least a few years ago, you're all set. If it happened more recently, pretend you're a bit older than you actually are; if you're only eighteen now, and this event happened last year, pretend you're looking back on the event from the grand old age of twenty-five.) What didn't you understand about the circumstances surrounding this event back when it happened? What didn't you understand about yourself? Perhaps what you did wasn't as bad as you've always thought it was and you can now forgive yourself for doing it. Or it was a lot worse than you've ever admitted and you can only now properly accept responsibility.

Think of at least one new way of looking at what you did. Now tell the same events as above, also in the first person ("I"), but in the past tense, from the vantage of this older, wiser self. Don't be afraid to allow your narrator to come right out and judge/analyze what happened and why. Usually, the older narrator speaks at the start of the story or the start of a new scene then fades out and simply recreates what happened from the perspective of the younger narrator.

If you like this exercise, you can repeat it for an event that required you to make a difficult choice or betray someone you love, or an event that was too complex for you to piece together or comprehend completely at the time.

LAURA KASISCHKE

LET THE DEAD SPEAK: AN EXERCISE IN FIRST-PERSON NARRATION

Laura Kasischke has published three novels, *Suspicious River*, *White Bird in a Blizzard*, and *The Life Before Her Eyes*. They have been translated widely and adapted for film. A young-adult novel, *Boy Heaven*, will be published next year. She has also published six collections of poetry and been the recipient of two fellowships from the National Endowment for the Arts and several Pushcart Prizes. She lives in Chelsea, Michigan, and teaches at the University of Michigan.

Contemporary fiction writers have been accused of choosing the first-person narrator for stories and novels because it's "easier." But most people who have written a story or a novel in the first person will tell you that the experience is a trying one—so many things to consider that can be overlooked when writing in the third person. Occasionally, however, the first person isn't a choice at all, it seems. Writers speak of being seized, inhabited, chosen by their narrators. They slip on their characters, their voices and sensibilities, the way an actor, or a medium, might.

The following exercise is an attempt to prime you for such a possibility, to help you set the stage for such an experience. Or set the table for such a guest to appear. The exercise privileges process over product, and although it doesn't require you to believe in a hereafter in which the dead are trying to contact the living (surely they've found better things to do?), it does help if you have at least some respect for the subconscious. Bob Marley said that the songs are just out there in the atmosphere, waiting for someone to hear them, to write them. Similarly, but less beautifully, when we were in sixth or seventh grade, we used to believe that those voices you can sometimes hear on the phone line, whispering under the conversation you actually called your friend to have, were the voices of the dead. Or, we didn't actually believe it, we liked to pretend we believed it. And why not? The idea that the dead still have things to say, and that some instrument might be able to pick up those stories, is a wonderful idea—the belief in the possibility of receptivity, that words and music, experience and consciousness, travel, can be retrieved, can be transferred and, maybe, rendered immortal, by teenagers on telephones, or writers at their desks.

This exercise proposes that story-writing might be the invitation for those voices to speak, and that the writer might be that instrument with which to pick them up—and that listening, then hearing, is an approach to writing in the first person that may result in authentic and energetic narration, rather than the bland pseudo-self writers have been accused of resorting to when they fall back on the first person.

EXERCISE

Conjure a ghost. Imagine a speaker, someone who has died (today? a thousand years ago?) without having had the opportunity to tell his or her story. This speaker is out there, choosing you. Your goal is to make yourself available for this storyteller. It's been my experience that the writers who are most successful with this exercise find speakers who, although not exactly like themselves, have some similar preoccupations or conflicts. Your ghost's troubles need not necessarily be yours, but it might help if they resonated. (Jack Kerouac said, "Things do not connect; they correspond . . . That is how we dead men write to each other.")

Now, spend a day or two thinking about your first-person narrator. What might she have enjoyed in her spare time? What would he like for dinner if he were to be invited from the other world to a dinner party in this one? A clearer picture should develop of your speaker before you can actually hear the voice. Do some research on your speaker's time period. Or go to the cemetery where he or she might be buried. If you're very brave, go at night. You will begin the actual writing of the story by imagining this ghost's voice speaking to or through you. It will require really listening, and trying to set your own voice aside in order to let this other's come through. Preferably, this is a ghost with an important story to tell, one he or she, perhaps, did not have the skill or the time to tell in life. Think of some questions for your ghost, and let the ghost speak.

A caveat: No matter how skeptical you are, try to make yourself believe that there is something eerie, unearthly, magnificent and transcendent, of you and apart from you, potentially traveling toward you as you travel toward it, and that this is your narrator, and your narrator's story. It's out there, and will be grateful for the invitation, and bring you a story.

Two gorgeous models for this: "Reassurance," by Allan Gurganus, a story in which a dead soldier writes to his mother, offering reassurance to her (inspired by a real letter from Walt Whitman), and Dan Chaon's story, "Sophomore, 19, Is School Year's First Fatality," from the point of view of the first college sophomore of the year to die in a drunk driving incident (inspired, apparently, by the newspaper headline which is the story's title).

CHARACTER DEVELOPMENT

EMPATHY AND THE
CREATION OF CHARACTER

Kay Sloan is a novelist, poet, and cultural historian. Her novels include *Worry Beads*, winner of the Ohioana Award for Best Fiction, and *The Patron Saint of Red Chevys*, selected as a Barnes & Noble Discover Great New Writers Book. Her book of poetry, *The Birds Are on Fire*, is the winner of the New Women's Voices Award from Finishing Line Press. She coauthored the book *Looking Far North: The Harriman Expedition to Alaska, 1899*. Sloan also produced and directed a documentary, *Suffragettes in the Silent Cinema*. She teaches at the European Center at Miami University in Oxford, Ohio.

Beginning writers are often told to write from their own experience, to "write what you know." But an essential element of writing is the understanding of what makes other people "tick," what motivates the actions of our characters. It is essential that we get outside of our selfhood, our pasts, and let loose our imagination.

This exercise asks that you make a leap into someone else's psyche and write from their point of view. Though our temptation as writers is often to write in an effort to explain ourselves, our past, our view of the world, one of the greatest rewards of reading fiction is understanding the whole cast of characters and what motivates their reactions to the world they live in. Since human nature is somewhat mysterious, the following "exchange" of yourself with someone else helps to penetrate that mystery a bit.

EXERCISE

- Spend a few moments thinking about a conflict that you have had with someone, whether a bus driver, a store clerk, or someone closer, a parent, a lover, a classmate from childhood. Write about what happened and why, how you felt, how the other person looked, what you remember about the place this occurred. What would you tell this person now so that he or she might understand you better?

- Once you have completed this, turn those sheets of paper over, or otherwise put them away. Turn to a fresh page. Close your eyes and now spend some time imagining that you are the person with whom you had the conflict. If you know the name of the person, write "My name is ____ and this is what happened." Then proceed to write from this person's point of view. What are you wearing? What do you see in the face of the other person (your real self)? How do you feel, in the "skin" of this person? Angry, hurt, happy? Why? What happened to you on that day or night? How would you describe the scene? What do you see, smell, or feel? What would you remember about what occurred and why? How were you changed by this conflict? Imagine your background, your history, what may have happened to you that day, good or bad, that only you know about? And what would you—as this other person—have to tell your real self about your role in the conflict?

The object of this exercise is to get outside of ourselves and empathize with someone whose point of view was or is greatly different from our own. This way, we can see ourselves as yet another character acting in the world, and get more in touch with the person that we are. It also helps us to see the many dimensions of a conflict and the complicated ways we react to one another.

Everyone is a character with motivations both good and bad—including us.

WHAT'S UNDER THE SURFACE?

Michelle Herman is the author of *Missing, A New and Glorious Life, The Middle of Everything*, and *Dog*. She teaches in the creative-writing program at Ohio State University. Her many awards and honors include the Harold U. Ribalow Award from Hadassah, grants from the National Endowment for the Arts and the Ohio Arts Council, and a James Michener Fellowship.

This is a very simple—deceptively simple—exercise that gets to the root of understanding character, which is itself at the root of writing fiction. Character (as you have no doubt been told many times by now) *is* story. If a writer puts characters through their paces—*making* them do things rather than allowing the things they do to arise in some organic way from *who they are*—then a story will not seem real; if a writer "gives" a character thoughts (as in, "Oops, I forgot to put in what she's *thinking* here—better do that!") but the thinking isn't anchored in the deeper recesses of that character's psyche, then the story won't seem real. And although good readers read for many things—the beauty of the language, the writer's wisdom and vision, the glimpse of a world not his own (and readers of every stripe read also simply to find out what happens next)—the secret of making narrative fiction that engages the reader is this: *make it real.* For if a story doesn't create the illusion of reality for its readers, it won't matter what the characters are up to, how much the writer knows about any particular thing, what her vision of the world is, what her ideas are, how cleverly constructed the story is, or how lovely or precise the language.

Why do we read fiction at all? is a question worth asking. It seems to me that the answer is as complicated as we humans are; but at the deepest level, it is because of our own longing to understand our humanness, to get beyond our limited understanding of our own single selves. When we step into a work of fiction we have the chance to do just that. But we have to believe in it for this understanding to occur, and for us to believe in it, it has to be as complicated and multilayered as we are, in "real" life.

EXERCISE

Think of something, anything at all, that one person might do to or with another. Slap his face. Bake her a cake. Take hold of her hand. Trip him as he walks by. Give her an expensive gift when it's not her birthday. Leave a nasty anonymous note under the windshield of her car. Or argue at top volume. Play Scrabble, or Monopoly. Go for a drive. In other words, truly anything—anything at all—that can transpire between human beings.

Now:

1. Write—briefly, in summary—what's happening. Describe it as if you are watching it, as if you have no idea why it's happening (which, at this point, you don't). All you know is what you can see, or surmise from what you can see. You may find it helpful, however, to name the people involved. "The man" and "the woman" or "the two girls" can get quickly tiresome. No more than a few sentences will be necessary, but be precise and concrete in what you do describe.

For example, *Nick and Karen were playing Monopoly. They had been playing for a long time, sitting on the floor. There was a fat stack of money and rows of neatly ordered property cards on Nick's side of the board, but Karen had Boardwalk and Park Place. A bowl with a few potato chips left in it was on the floor beside them, and two bottles of beer. Karen's was almost empty.*

2. Choose one of your characters and perform surgery: slit open his or her mind and enter it. See what you find in there that is *of the moment*—that is, self-reflective, but also self-contained. Don't try to cover every possible thought the character could be having at such a moment. Just choose one line and follow it through:

    Karen was a little drunk, she suspected, though she'd only had three-quarters of a bottle of beer. But she felt funny—she felt silly, really. She wasn't used to drinking. She tried to make herself feel serious as she picked up the dice and shook them, but she must have looked as silly as she felt, because Nick started to laugh.

3. Now step back from this, get out another piece of paper, and ask yourself this series of questions, which you should answer thoughtfully, but without worrying about your choice of words—at this point you are not writing so much as *thinking* on paper.

Why are these characters doing what they're doing right now?
    In this case, why are Karen and Nick playing Monopoly, and why are they drinking beer? Why is Nick laughing?

Why is my protagonist (the one who's doing the thinking) thinking what she's thinking?
    This may seem difficult, but it will seem more manageable if you

add "why" to every thought you've allowed her to have. Answer the question as completely as you can. Next, you will want to slip beneath the "why." For example, if you've answered the question *Why does Karen feel she has to seem "serious"?* by jotting down the note *Because she admires Nick and wants him to take her seriously; she always feels a little stupid and goofy around him,* then you must ask yourself both *Why does she admire Nick?* And *What makes her feel stupid around him?* And you must continue this line of inquiry until you have reached a dead end (*She admires him because he is smart and self-confident; he's also good-looking* will lead to *What makes her think he's smart?* and *Does she think he's smarter than she is? Is this actually true?* If the answer to *Is this actually true?* is *No, she just feels this way, she feels inferior to him,* then you must ask yourself, *Why does Karen feel so inferior? What made her that way?*)

At any point in this process you can go back to the original scenario and add an exchange of dialogue (*"What?" Karen said. "Nothing," Nick told her, but he was still laughing*) and repeat Step 2—and then Step 3—to yield more information about the character doing the thinking here.

What's the point of all this? To give you practice in asking questions about your own characters, so that you can understand them as fully as possible—so that you know "where they're coming from" at any given moment. It may surprise you how much you "know" about someone you've just invented on a lark.

This process of asking why and then why again will help you to find out more about your characters than you had imagined you knew. It's all there—all the information is always there—locked inside you. You just need to find ways to coax it out and onto the page.

LAUREN GRODSTEIN

THE INTERVIEW

Lauren Grodstein is the author of the short-story collection *The Best of Animals* and the novel *Reproduction Is the Flaw of Love*. Her essays, stories, and reviews have appeared in various publications, including *Virgin Fiction 2*, *The Modern Jewish Girl's Guide to Guilt*, *The New York Times*, and the *Ontario Review*. A graduate of Columbia University's MFA program, Grodstein teaches creative writing at Rutgers University. She lives in Brooklyn, New York.

T he stories and novels that I write are usually pretty interior— the characters tend to drive the action, instead of the other way around. I've found that the best way, then, for me to write convincing stories is to create characters who are as human as I can make them. For instance, my novel, *Reproduction Is the Flaw of Love,* is about a young man who waits outside the bathroom door while his girlfriend takes a pregnancy test. The entire thing takes place in the narrative space of an hour and a half (give or take a few flashbacks). Without a compelling character with whom to wait outside that bathroom door, the reader would quickly lose interest in the story. So, when I was writing *Reproduction,* I did everything I could to make Miller, my hero, as three-dimensional as he could possibly be. I wrote interior monologues for him, devised his family tree, wrote scenes from his childhood, and, finally, interviewed him.

To be honest, I forget where I got the idea of interviewing a character—although I'm certain I didn't make it up—but doing it allowed me to get to know Miller more intimately than I might have otherwise. I trained myself to hear his voice. I learned that he's a quiet guy, although he'll speak in long, rambling sentences when he's feeling philosophical. I learned that he likes to listen to classical music, but only by himself, in a car on a country road. I learned that he's suspicious of cats. And, most important, I learned to see him as an individual, instead of just an extension of myself, the writer.

Interviewing characters is not necessarily a surefire way to start writing three-dimensional people; it can feel forced or silly, and sometimes just like extra work a writer doesn't need. But I've gotten hooked on it. It helps me know my characters better, and spend some time with them outside the limited confines of the novel or story to which they belong. And that, in itself, is a pleasure.

Often, writers feel the urge to write about characters who are really thinly veiled versions of themselves. (Some authors simply get right to it and baldly name their characters after themselves; the star of Philip Roth's *Operation Shylock,* for example, is a novelist named Philip Roth.) I recommend that you avoid this urge if possible. First, it's not such a stretch to write about someone who has the same job as you, uses the same toothpaste, wears the same sneakers. Second, there's often a falseness or a forcedness apparent in characters who are clearly too close to the author. It's as though by writing about versions of themselves, the authors become more concerned with "getting it right" than with good writing. The author becomes so obsessed with describing his own day at work, getting the details perfectly, that he forgets that he's writing fiction.

So instead of writing about yourself (or your father, or your wife) try instead to write about a purely invented character. The inspiration for this character can come from anywhere, but the details of his or her life should come from your imagination. Think carefully: What does your character look like? Bald spot? Glasses? What motivates him to go to work every day (or not go to work every day)? Where did he go to school? What were his parents like? Is he a cat person? Dog person? Parakeet person? Vegetarian? Even if none of these details are relevant to the story, you need to know them to convince your reader of the genuineness of your fictional world. A thin character is not strong enough to hold up the narrative dream your stories should create.

EXERCISE

This assignment involves creating a character and getting to know that character as well as you can. Your job is to interview your character as though you were a journalist for, say, *Esquire* or *The New Yorker,* and your character were the subject of a big juicy profile piece. Here are some of the questions you might want to ask your character:

— What is your earliest childhood memory?

— What's your idea of a dream vacation?

— If you could have any other job, what would it be?

— Whom do you consider a hero?

— Which do you prefer: rock, opera, or jazz—and why?

— Or do you only listen to talk radio? Or do you listen to nothing at all?

Ask your interviewee anything you want!

"ONCE UPON A TIME": PLAYING WITH TIME IN FICTION

Elizabeth Graver is the author of three novels, *Awake, The Honey Thief*, and *Unravelling*, and the story collection *Have You Seen Me?* Her writing has been anthologized in *The Best American Short Stories*; *The O. Henry Prize Stories*; *The Best American Essays*; and *The Pushcart Prize* anthology. She teaches at Boston College.

This exercise uses a classic fairy tale, "Little Red Riding Hood," as a springboard for exploring how experimenting with time in fiction can help you explore your characters in more depth.

THE STORY

Once upon a time, there lived a woodcutter and his wife, who had one little girl. In the next village lived her old grandmother, who loved her so much that she made a nice scarlet hood for her to keep her warm. When the neighbors saw it, they called her "Little Red Riding Hood," and after a time, no one ever thought to call her by any other name.

One day her mother said to her, "Granny has been very ill. Put on your hood and take her these cheesecakes that I have made for her." Little Red Riding Hood started off and soon came to a wood that lay between the two villages. Just then a wolf, who was passing, saw Red Riding Hood and said, "Where are you going, Red Riding Hood?"

"I am going to see my grandmother, Mr. Wolf," answered the little girl.

"Where does she live?" asked the wolf.

"Oh, she lives in the first cottage past yonder mill. She is very ill, so I am taking her these cheesecakes."

"If she is so ill, I will go and see her too," said the wolf. "I will go this way, and you go through the wood, and we will see who gets there first." So saying, he shambled off and then ran all the way to the cottage. Tap, tap—he knocked at the cottage door.

"Who is there?" asked the grandmother.

"It is I," answered the wolf, in a soft voice, "Little Red Riding Hood; I have brought you nice fresh cakes."

"Pull the bobbin and the latch will lift up," called out the grandmother. And the wolf pulled the bobbin, lifted the latch, and entered the cottage. He ate up the poor grandmother, put on her nightgown, pulled her nightcap right over his ugly rough head, and got into bed. "The old lady was tough," he said, "but the girl will be a delicate morsel."

But little Red Riding Hood lingered on in the wood, gathering posies for her old grandmother, who could not get out and see the spring flowers grow. At last, tired with her play, she set off to reach her grandmother's cottage. She knocked at the door, and the wolf, softening his voice, called out, "Pull the bobbin, and the latch will go up." Red Riding Hood opened the door and walked in.

"Put the basket on the table, and come into bed with me," said the wolf, "for I feel cold."

Little Red Riding Hood thought that her grandmother's voice was very hoarse, but then she remembered that this might be on account of her cold, and being an obedient girl, she got into bed. But when she saw the hairy arms, she began to grow frightened. "What long arms you have, Grandmother!"

"The better to hug you with, my dear."

Then she saw the long ears sticking up outside the nightcap. "What great ears you have, Grandmother!"

"The better to hear you with, my dear."

"What large eyes you have, Grandmother!"

"The better to see you with, my dear."

"What great teeth you have, Grandmother!"

"The better to eat you with, my darling," shouted the wolf, and with one bound, he sprang out of bed and would have gobbled Red Riding Hood right up, had she not been too quick.

She ran screaming out of the cottage. Fortunately Karl, the woodman's son, was passing, and he quickly killed the wolf with his axe. Little Red Riding Hood was very much frightened but not hurt. Karl took her home to her mother, and after that day, she was not allowed to go through the wood alone.

EXERCISE

Write on from where the ellipses end. Spend around ten minutes on each of the four sections, or more if you're so inspired.

1. First person, Subjective Time, where you imagine your way inside Red Riding Hood's voice, thoughts and experiences.

    "What great teeth you have, Grandmother!"
    "The better to eat you with, my darling," shouted the wolf, and with one bound, he sprang out of bed and would have gobbled me right up, had not I been too quick. I ran screaming out of the cottage, and as I ran, all my fears ran close behind. I saw . . .

2. Future Time, where you project Red Riding Hood forward, far into the future:

Little Red Riding Hood was very much frightened but not hurt.
Karl took her home to her mother, and after that day she was not
allowed to go through the wood alone. What she could not know
then, but would learn many years later, after she had a daughter
of her own, was that . . .

3. Animal Time, where you imagine the perspective of an
   animal, who lives outside of human "clock time" and very
   much inside sensation.

   Little Red Riding Hood lingered on in the wood, gathering posies
   for her old grandmother, who could not get out and see the spring
   flowers grow. At last, tired with her play, she set off to reach her
   grandmother's cottage. While the girl played, the wolf shambled
   off through the forest. His legs felt . . .

4. The Grandmother's Time, or Time Collapsing, where you
   explore how, in the grip of a strong emotion, a character's
   experiences of time can become particularly jumbled and
   complex.

   "Pull the bobbin and the latch will lift up," called out the grand-
   mother. And the wolf pulled the bobbin, lifted the latch, and en-
   tered the cottage . . ." Now the grandmother had lived for ninety
   years and had seen a great many things. What happened to her
   next threw her back upon her past, flung her far into the future,
   and froze her solidly in place, all at precisely the same time.
   She . . .

ROBERT ANTHONY SIEGEL

WHY I STOLE IT

Robert Anthony Siegel believes that good fiction is always driven by emotion. He is the author of the novel *All the Money in the World* and teaches at the University of North Carolina at Wilmington.

One of the very difficult things in fiction is creating characters who are active rather than passive—who act on their desires rather than simply thinking about them. There are, in fact, two parts to this problem: the first part is identifying a single clear desire that motivates your character; the second part is discovering an action that both derives from that desire and embodies it in a complex and meaningful way. The exercise "Why I Stole It" offers a means to explore both sides of the desire/action equation.

EXERCISE

To begin, go through your house and find an object that interests you. It might be offbeat, like a souvenir from a Florida alligator farm, or it might be ordinary, like a wooden mixing spoon. Then sit down with the object in front of you and have your character explain in her own words why she stole it.

"Why I Stole It" is a versatile exercise. You can use it to better understand a character you are already dealing with or you can use it to create a new character—for example, the lovesick baker who stole the mixing spoon. And after you have written about the baker's reason for stealing the spoon, you can go on to explore all the other things that follow from it: whom she stole it from; how she stole it; what happened after she stole it; whom she is now confessing to; and why she is confessing.

CHRIS ABANI

LANGUAGE PORTRAIT

Chris Abani's prose includes the novels *GraceLand* and *Masters of the Board* and a novella, *Becoming Abigail*. His poetry collections are *Hands Washing Water, Dog Woman, Daphne's Lot,* and *Kalakuta Republic.* He is an associate professor at the University of California, Riverside, and teaches in the MFA Program at Antioch University, Los Angeles. He is the recipient of the 2001 PEN USA Freedom-to-Write Award, the 2001 Prince Claus Award, a 2003 Lannan Literary Fellowship, and the 2005 PEN/Hemingway Book Prize.

In nineteenth-century England, the newspapers published "language portraits," often by popular writers like Dickens.

EXERCISE

Write a language portrait using words to describe a place or person as vividly as a photograph would, staying away from obvious physical descriptions, and easy action. Search instead for details like the buttons on a coat, the smell of oregano coming in a window, dentures—combine these with the essence of your character. For example: The smell of oregano wafted through the screen door on hot summer afternoons as Granny smacked toothless gums together,

her dentures resting in a glass beside her, as she readied herself for her afternoon nap."

This often leads to surprising and interesting turns and developments for the character we are working on and helps to flesh her out better for the reader. It enables the reader to place his own associations onto the character, to find his way into the story that way.

RACHEL BASCH

PAW THROUGH THEIR POCKETS, RIFLE THROUGH THEIR DRAWERS: A CHARACTER EXERCISE

Rachel Basch is the author of two novels, *The Passion of Reverend Nash* and *Degrees of Love*. She is a visiting writer at Trinity College in Hartford, Connecticut.

I n *Rabbit Is Rich,* Harry Angstrom catalogs every square inch of Cindy Murkett's bathroom, as if the decor was a means for decoding this woman he lusts after. But it is the contents of Cindy's medicine cabinet that yield the unexpected nugget of her secret self. In a list that takes up nearly a page in the novel, Updike enumerates with exquisite specificity the lotions, ointments, creams and prescriptions on the shelves. Harry exits the bathroom with the conclusion that "(m)edicine cabinets are tragic."

Medicine cabinets are also mysterious, ironic, emblematic, comic, idiosyncratic, ambiguous, contradictory, compelling, horrifying, seductive . . . And the same can be said for the contents of a purse, a wallet, a gym bag, backpack, glove compartment, refrigerator, pantry, desk drawer, nightstand, school locker, briefcase, safety deposit box, jewelry box . . .

Nothing is more essential to the process of writing fiction than knowing your character from the inside out. So much of the work involves getting those characters to give over the goods, to uncover themselves, reveal the deep truths that allow us to identify, to recognize them as one of us. How do we move from the idea of a character—the superficials, the résumé, the outlines—to the creation of a person as palpable and animate as we are? Stuff. We look at their stuff. We paw through their pockets and rifle through their drawers.

EXERCISE

I've adapted this exercise from one of Richard Russo's exercises about developing character from place. Choose one of the containers mentioned above, a wallet, a jewelry box, etc., and simply make a list of what your character keeps there. Don't think about plot. This exercise is not concerned with planting information for later complications (though that may happen, subconsciously). What is key here is choosing the right items, ones that ring true for your character and ones that are painfully specific only to her. If her wallet contains ticket stubs, what were the performances? If there's a grocery list, what's on it? What's crossed off? Are there pay stubs, pawnshop claims, to-do lists, phone numbers, addresses, quotes, IOUs, lottery tickets, coupons, photos, ID cards, credit cards? How much money is in the wallet? In what denominations?

Try to stick to a simple enumeration at first, no lapsing into narrative explanations, digressions, flashbacks. Just the facts, the objects. The goal is to create an index of contents that in its entirety and specificity could belong to only one person—your character.

MR. SAMSA, MEET BARTLEBY

Maxine Chernoff is a professor and chair of the Creative Writing Program at San Francisco State University. With Paul Hoover, she edits the long-running literary journal *New American Writing*. She is the author of six books of fiction and eight books of poetry, most recently *Among the Names*. Her work has appeared in many magazines, including *Conjunctions, ZYZZYVA, The North American Review, Chicago Review, The Paris Review, Partisan Review, Sulfur, New Directions Annual, Denver Quarterly, Hambone, Slope*, and *Verse*. Her collection of stories, *Signs of Devotion*, was a New York Times Notable Book of 1993. Both her novel *American Heaven* and her book of short stories, *Some of Her Friends That Year*, were finalists for the Bay Area Book Reviewers Award. Her novel *A Boy in Winter* is currently in production in Canada by an independent film company.

Scenes between predictably similar people, couples in a relationship, mother and child, Dad with his drinking buddies, etc., often lead a writer to lazy results. The characters say what you expect them to say, and the scene or story becomes merely a journal. An interesting way to oppose this tendency is to get characters involved in discussion whose lives or current life situations are strongly discordant.

In several of my novels, I have imagined the outcome of, for instance, a newly arrived Polish mathematician whose new job in America is to care for an elderly African-American jazz musician

(*American Heaven*). In another book, a runaway teenager goes to see not her own neurotic, urban grandmother but the reticent, rural Native American grandmother of her mother's new boyfriend (*Plain Grief*). People are surprised by each other and end up exploring things about themselves and others that they wouldn't with more comfortable, known companions.

EXERCISE

A way to explore the situation of odd couples in a writing exercise is to "break and enter" literarily. What if Connie in "Where Are You Going, Where Have You Been?" were visited by the burly blind man in Raymond Carver's story "Cathedral" instead of the menacing Arnold Friend? What would she learn about herself from this calmer, safer, wiser presence? What if Bartleby the Scrivener had to spend a morning with Gregor Samsa? Would he be roused out of his self-indulgent lethargy? Would Gregor Samsa take comfort from such a visit? Would Gregor's father realize that there are worlds of unsuitable sons?

By joining characters from one story with those of another, you can learn to project other possibilities. You can imagine dialogue that you would otherwise never write. You can take yourself out of the limited confines of relationships you've explored or based too much on your own experience and imagine other worlds where speakers and listeners are paired to surprise you, the writer, into exercising your imagination beyond its favored territories and pathways.

I might begin such a story (two characters from different stories by different authors) by beginning a dialogue between them and seeing what they have to say to each other. Another possibility would be to insert a character from a known work of literature into your own existing plot. A bored Mom and Dad are sitting with their morning coffee around the kitchen table when Cousin Stanley

Kowalski comes to visit, fresh from losing Stella. Later you may name him something else if you wish, but you've moved your story beyond the usual breakfast by making him show up. Even very famous characters can suddenly enter your fiction. A Raskolnikov-like boy signs up for senior year at your main character's high school. Given his interests and "predilections," what will your protagonist do to keep history from repeating itself?

Your responsibility as a writer is to use not only your own limited experience but what literature gives you to create new moments of tension, passion, humor, and complication.

MICHELLE BROOKS

RATTLESNAKE IN THE DRAWER

Michelle Brooks is the author of *Such Short Supply*, a book of poetry. Her fiction has been published in *Alaska Quarterly Review*, *Blue Mesa Review*, *Hayden's Ferry Review*, *Orchid*, *The Baltimore Review*, and *Parting Gifts*. Her poetry has appeared in *The Madison Review*, *Phoebe*, *The Saint Ann's Review*, *Eclipse*, *Natural Bridge*, *Slipstream*, *HazMat Review*, *Poetry Motel*, *Spire Press*, *Nerve Cowboy*, *New Zoo Poetry Review*, *Revolve*, *The Circle*, *Long Shot*, *Poetrybay*, and *Gargoyle*. She has a doctorate in creative writing from the University of North Texas. She won the *Ledge* poetry chapbook contest in 2004 for *No Half-Measures Here* and the *Nerve Cowboy* poetry chapbook contest in the same year for *A Hotel Room in Baton Rouge*.

While living in an old house on a ranch, my friend Mark found a small rattlesnake coiled in his dresser drawer. Hoping to pull out a T-shirt and go to sleep, he was forced to reevaluate his setting and act accordingly. Mark fears snakes and loves guns, so he pulled out his pump shotgun and aimed at the snake. The dresser didn't survive, but the snake slithered by into parts unknown. Mark suffered through several restless nights, wondering where the snake had gone and if it would return. As writers, we can imagine many objects that would act like rattlesnakes and several potential reactions to those threats.

EXERCISE

In this exercise, imagine a specific character going about his or her mundane daily tasks and finding something unexpected that brings about a strong reaction. This should be a physical object that creates either a physical or mental threat, or a mystery, real or imagined. The "rattlesnake" must be something that could feasibly be found in one of the rooms of the house and has the power to unsettle your character and change the course of his or her trajectory in the scene you are writing. For example, you could imagine a wife who had a hysterectomy many years ago finding a box of condoms while cleaning her husband's bathroom. There could be several explanations for this object and many ways that she could react to it. The more fully imagined the scene is, the deeper the writer can delve into the mystery of the life that is being changed in some subtle or dramatic way.

Pick a room from the following list: bathroom, kitchen, living room, closet, basement, garage, attic. The more specific you can make your details, the better. The end result of this exercise should be a better understanding of the ways that a specific setting detail can help you write your character more fully and impose external pressure on your story.

A FAMILY THEME,
A FAMILY SECRET

K. L. Cook is the author of *Last Call*, a collection of linked stories that won the inaugural Prairie Schooner Book Prize in Fiction, and the novel *The Girl from Charnelle*. He teaches creative writing and literature at Prescott College in Arizona and at Spalding University in Louisville, Kentucky, in the MFA in Writing Program.

In addition to teaching a variety of creative-writing workshops, I also co-teach Family Systems in Film and Literature, an interdisciplinary literature/psychology course in which we use stories, novellas, and films to illuminate the complex emotional legacies within families. In a family biography assignment, I ask students to write a narrative that examines a particular issue, theme, pattern, or secret within their own families.

This assignment often provokes the most compelling, eloquent, and psychologically complex narratives I've read from students, even from students who don't necessarily consider themselves writers. The assignment has been so successful that I've adapted it for my fiction-writing workshops, often with extraordinary results. I particularly like how the exercise encourages writers to move beyond simplistic depictions of characters (and families of characters) as victims and victimizers. Instead, it urges writers to examine the way a whole group contributes to a theme or secret, as well as the way that a theme or secret can clarify the identity, values, emotional history, desires, and anxieties of the family. This assignment has also deeply informed the writing and revision of my own books—*Last Call*, a short story cycle that depicts three generations in the life of a West Texas family, and *The Girl from Charnelle*, a novel that focuses on a series of interlocking secrets in this same family.

EXERCISE

Family Themes. Predominant themes emerge over generations and are imprinted on a family as a kind of private mythology. "I come from a family of honorable thieves," a character might say. Or, as Nick Carraway announces at the beginning of *The Great Gatsby*, "My family have been prominent, well-to-do people in this middle-western city for three generations . . . and we have a tradition that we are descended from the Dukes of Buccleuch . . ."

Focus on a central theme in your fictional family's life. From where does this theme seem to derive? How has this theme worked through the generations, positively and/or negatively? In what ways has it helped create a sense of loyalty and identity among the family members, and in what ways has it agitated the chronic anxiety and led to cut-off, regression, or reinvention? Keep in mind that with a family theme, the family members are not only consciously but often keenly aware of the theme and its emotional legacy. Once you've established this theme, try one of the following narrative strategies:

1. Create a scene in which two characters from the family are at odds about the legitimacy of this family theme. Let one character attempt to convince the other to follow a destiny that will either reinforce or break free from this theme. Have the other character resist those arguments.

2. Structure a story around three family members. Let one family member passionately attempt to convince a second (your protagonist) to follow or live by the family theme/legacy, and let a third family member attempt to convince the second to resist, even undermine, the family theme/legacy. (It helps to let the two members of the family who are trying to convince the protagonist have histories which reinforce their positions.)

Family Secrets. According to family systems theory, there are no secrets in families. The entire family colludes, either consciously or unconsciously, in keeping and perpetuating a secret. Often a secret is linked to a family's conception of shame and may be used as a tool for one generation to exert its will (about how to behave) over another generation. For example, in Maxine Hong Kingston's essay, "No Name Woman," the suppression of a Chinese woman's shame and suicide creates anxiety not only in her entire family but especially in her niece (Kingston herself) as she searches for "ancestral help" in defining her own identity. In James Baldwin's story "Sonny's Blues," the narrator learns a terrible secret about his father and uncle that determines the way in which he tries to protect his brother.

Is there a secret in your fictional family? How has that secret generated either chronic or acute anxiety in the life of this family? Does that secret directly affect the story you wish to tell? Can you identify the members of this family who absorb or "bind" the anxiety of this suppressed secret? How do they bind it? What is the effect of the secret on the emotional health of the entire fictional family as well as the individuals within it?

Once you've explored the nuances of this secret, use it as the primary organizing strategy for your story. Here are two ways of doing this:

1. Start your story with a detailed accounting of the secret and then structure your narrative to dramatize the emotional

effects of this secret on the character most "bound" by the anxiety it creates.

2. Structure your story as a mystery in which you create a protagonist who, from the beginning of the narrative, is on a search to discover the secret and who must contend with various family members' attempts to either aid or sabotage this search. (A secret's power comes from its repression, and there will always be members of a family who want to either continue the suppression of the secret or expose it in order to strip it of its emotional power.)

MICHAEL DATCHER

CHARACTERS IN CONFLICT

Michael Datcher is the author of the *New York Times* best-seller *Raising Fences*. He is a professor of English at Loyola Marymount University in Los Angeles.

The complicated interaction between characters is what makes great writing engaging. This is especially true when characters are in conflict. However, it's rare for two characters to come into the conflict equally armed. Usually, one character is simply more compelling in presenting his or her case. In boxing, the most intriguing contests are between two fighters who are equally matched. The same can be said for characters in opposition. This exercise is designed to give the writer practice at creating two characters that are coming to the battle with equal ammunition. It draws from the writer's personal history with conflict and tries to place the writer in the mind of an opponent.

EXERCISE

Think of a time when you had a serious disagreement or argument with someone. One in which you felt the other party was certainly in the wrong. Now, write a letter, addressed to yourself, from the other person's perspective. In this letter, take on the voice of your adversary, as your adversary explains her perspective on why she was right and you were certainly in the wrong.

This exercise is a great way to practice writing from perspectives other than your own. It's also a good way to humanize antagonists.

THE VOYAGER: WRITE WHAT YOU DON'T KNOW: AN EXERCISE IN (SURPRISING YOURSELF WITH) CHARACTER

Edie Meidav is the author of the recent novel *Crawl Space*, winner of the Bard Fiction Prize, *The Far Field: A Novel of Ceylon*, winner of the Kafka Award for the best novel by an American woman, and has a novel-in-progress entitled *Highway Five*. Currently, she directs the MFA writing program at New College of California in San Francisco.

To get my California persona out front and open: *right now, all sorts of radiowaves are moving through your body.* Fictional, historical, poetic, linguistic radiowaves. Where you're sitting rests upon some kind of burial ground. Wherever you read these words, a flurry of gesture and conversation has taken place between a couple of somebodies, even if you huddle in the thick of a night-time forest and not in a dense café or subway car. Can we say that all prior and present conversations press into you, making delicate incursions upon your consciousness? To shift into another post-twentieth-century metaphor: imagine you are a bit of walking Velcro and have picked up the lint of thousands of gestures observed, conversations overheard, concepts misapprehended.

Once, I was on a boat leaving the Scottish port of Stornaway, sitting behind two men and one man said to the other: *Say what you will about the Jews, they do know how to*—and it doesn't even matter how the man finished the sentence. Already his ramrod neck and words had entered me into a different milieu, say, a golf club, in which no permission is ever needed to say *they do know how to.*

One reason I like writing novels is that I get to exit my own limited life and take on others' personas ("mask" in Greek). Under the masks, I've felt the greatest freedom and chance to live out—and learn about—subjectivities beyond my own limited sphere. How many people do you really claim to know well in your life? Thirty-six? Here is where invention comes into play: getting out of your own way, you stumble into a wealth of material.

The novelist Kazuo Ishiguro says he likes to write his novels first and then research later, finding often that what he has written is true to life. Perhaps for many of us, too much research beforehand can foreclose the possibilities of the imagination and may also be a sophisticated form of procrastination. Similarly, Stephen Crane wrote *The Red Badge of Courage* before he'd ever stepped onto a battlefield. When he became a soldier, he discovered that he'd instinctively known everything he ended up experiencing. A creative hypothesis forming the result of the experiment? Maybe. Yet what's to lose if you dare a bit?

What I have seen with writing students over many years is that it takes the slightest little jar to get them onto the boat from Stornaway, into all the magical tangents leading out from their own autobiographies. A little cognitive disturbance seems to help. In the silver-tongued parlance of American used-car dealers, my guarantee for this exercise is this: at least a few moments of transport.

EXERCISE

Try visiting a café or a bus station, an airport departure lounge or a hospital's waiting room, a gambling precinct or bar—in other words, any zone where people enter a state of suspension, waiting for the next bit of life to move them an inch farther toward their goals or mortality. Choose a person near you who won't notice your gaze. Jot down, quickly, your imagined sense of this person's:

1. attitude in relation to authority figures

2. perfect mate

3. biggest shame

4. ideal job vs. actual job

5. first moment of childhood happiness

6. peak romantic experience s/he is constantly trying to re-create

7. bed

8. refrigerator's innards

9. nervous tics

10. dream life

11. biggest rival/antagonist

12. desired tribe/community vs. actual tribe/community

13. biggest accomplishment s/he wishes to achieve

14. favorite site of refuge and succor

15. person from the past s/he doesn't wish to bump into

16. most challenging physical act

17. most challenging mental act

18. most challenging emotional act: e.g., forgiveness, revelation, self-recognition.

19. desired resting ground

Note to the adventurous: What happens if you transpose some of these details to a different social or historical milieu? If you are in San Francisco in the early part of this century, what would happen if you saw, for example, your character as a betrayed minstrel in the 1600s? An intrepid moon settler in the 2200s?

Now (with a nod toward John Gardner) give yourself twenty minutes—no more than twenty minutes—to write in the voice of your character, using the first-person voice after s/he has witnessed a murder.

See what surprises you. Whatever surprises you will surprise your reader. And what surprises you may lead into a longer work rising from the simple inspiration of your voyager.

Surprise = your key into the rosy realms.

GETTING DRAMATIC

Joan Silber is the author of *Ideas of Heaven: A Ring of Stories*, selected in 2004 as a finalist for the National Book Award and the Story Prize. Her four other books of fiction are *Lucky Us, In My Other Life, In the City*, and *Household Words*, winner of a PEN/ Hemingway Award. Her work has been chosen for *The O. Henry Prize Stories* and *The Pushcart Prize Anthology* and has appeared in *The New Yorker, Ploughshares, The Paris Review*, and other magazines. She has received awards from the Guggenheim Foundation, the National Endowment for the Arts, and the New York Foundation for the Arts. She lives in New York City and teaches at Sarah Lawrence College.

EXERCISE

Ask three people: "What's the most dramatic thing that has ever happened to you?"

Pick one answer and write a scene about that event.

I came up with this assignment because so much student writing seems stuck in the pedestrian. But it made me think, What does anyone mean by "dramatic"? Technically, a drama is a serious (non-comic) play; the need to act out feelings on the stage has probably led to its secondary meaning, which is high emotion. At my friends' kid's nursery school, they say, "Save the drama for your mama," and even the four-year-olds know what this means.

In fiction, the writer's job is to make sure events are fully dramatized, that enough happens so that we feel what the writer wants us to. (And writers can also overdramatize events—there can be too much action and not enough meaning.) The what's-at-stake question, so common in workshops, is closely connected to the question of what's-the-drama. Getting someone else's report on an experience of the "dramatic" can raise the stakes from the get-go. Answers involve trauma, risk, pride, shame, heartbreak.

Aristotle, always thinking about drama, said a tragedy was an imitation of an action of high importance, complete in itself and rendered so that the viewer, through pity and fear, experienced catharsis. Modern short stories do this in their own ways. This assignment, though it's only an exercise, is meant to remind writers of that purpose. It also gets them out of their own experience, which can be a good thing.

MARY YUKARI WATERS

DEVELOPING YOUR
CHARACTERS

Mary Yukari Waters has been anthologized in *The Best American Short Stories 2002, 2003*, and *2004; The O. Henry Prize Stories; The Pushcart Prize*; Francis Ford Coppola's *Zoetrope: All-Story 2*; and *The Pushcart Book of Short Stories: The Best Short Stories from a Quarter-Century of the Pushcart Prize*. She is the recipient of a grant from the National Endowment for the Arts, and her fiction has aired on NPR's *Selected Shorts* and on BBC Radio. Her debut collection, *The Laws of Evening*, was a Book Sense 76 selection and a selection for the Barnes & Noble Discover Great New Writers program. It was also selected as a Kiriyama Prize Notable Book. *Newsday* and the *San Francisco Chronicle* chose *The Laws of Evening* as one of the Best Books of 2003. She received her MFA from the University of California and lives in Los Angeles.

I once saw a wonderful Japanese film called *Afterlife*. The movie's premise was that after you die, you have three days of limbo in which to choose one memory from your life to take with you to the afterlife. All other memories will be erased. There were several characters in this film, all trying to choose among memories. I was surprised at how well I felt I understood these characters, even though I knew nothing else about them except the memories they ultimately chose. Afterward, I tried to figure out what my own happiest memory was. I realized, after a lot of thought, that it wasn't going to be one of the "obvious" moments, like graduating or winning a prize or having a great party. I actually wonder if I've forgotten my happiest moment, that it was too fleeting and not connected to a big memorable event.

At any rate, this inspired an exercise that I sometimes give my students when they're having a hard time turning a one-dimensional character into a three-dimensional one.

EXERCISE

Try to figure out which memory that character might choose, if he was forced to. Go beyond what seems obvious; take your time and really give it some serious thought. It's not necessary to include any of this in your actual story. Just do it on the side, when you've hit a wall in your character development. It will give you new insights into your character, and reveal some intriguing emotional layers that you never suspected were there.

LISE HAINES

THE WAY THEY DO THE THINGS THEY DO

Lise Haines is the author of the novel *In My Sister's Country.* Her second novel, tentatively titled *Small Acts of Sex and Electricity*, will be published in fall 2006. She is writer in residence at Emerson College and has been a finalist for the PEN/Nelson Algren Fiction Award and the Patterson Fiction Prize. Her short stories and essays have appeared in journals including *Ploughshares*, *AGNI*, and *Post Road Magazine*. Haines lives in Massachusetts.

My landlord called one day to say she had scheduled maintenance on my chimney. This was a new ritual for me. In all the apartments I had lived in, I couldn't recall a single moment of de-sooting. In that way that writers have of ramping up on small events, my mind launched into a series of quirky images. At the appointed hour a guy would knock on my newly painted door, leaving his black knuckle-shaped prints in evidence. He would push his way into my living room and drop a dusty bag on my buff carpet and tell a couple of off-color *Mary Poppins* jokes. After slugging back the coffee and tea cookies I offer all my research subjects, he'd get to work, penetrating the inner reaches of the chimney. The noise he'd make would be equal in ferocity to a lumber truck coursing downhill on worn brakes. The work, as I saw it, would send an atomic cloud of soot into the apartment, permeating my couch cushions and lingering in my linen closet. All of my cereals and crackers would suffer contamination, and there would be weeks of inhaling a scent akin to stale campground.

When the actual chimney sweep arrived, I invited in a tidy individual named Dave. I watched him cover a small area in clean plastic and run a machine like an industrial vacuum cleaner. He had a set of well-worn brushes lined up like croquet mallets in a rack and a bag full of black hoses that hooked together with brass couplings. I saw no grim clouds, and I could have gone off to my desk and worked, for all the excitement.

Instead, I got curious. I asked Dave if he wouldn't mind telling me about the various brushes. I asked what I should do when I'd had my fire for the evening, and wanted to go off to sleep, and the coals were still going. Dousing them with water is not the right answer. I wanted to know if I would be better off buying a face cord or a full cord, and if the pine that was cut and stacked near the garage was a reasonable wood to burn. What I found, as I do with most people who are expert at something: Dave was more than happy to talk. He embellished his answers with the kind of detail you can't readily find using the straightforward tools of the Info Age. He handed over personal anecdotes saved up from thirty years in the profession. During the length of one short interrogation, I had a workable fireplace, a heads up on how not to burn the house down, and enough material to start a short story.

EXERCISE

Think of someone you know who has an expertise. Any passion qualifies. She might know about sailing catamarans or how to prepare a canvas for oil paint. You could find someone who understands medicinal herbs, or why some people choose drywall over plaster when renovating an old house. You might simply call on a willing relative to discuss his technique for making a light cruller.

Next, set up an informal interview. Whether you do this in person or over the phone, the essential thing is to be inquisitive. Ask a great number of questions and when you get answers, go for details. Give your subject ample time to tell his/her personal stories. Take notes.

Once you're at your computer or have your notebook in hand, write down ten things you've learned in simple, declarative sentences. Look over your list and find the line that would make the most compelling first line to a short story. See the character that *needs* to convey this information. Now write a first-person story in your character's voice starting with your first line.

In workshop

I ask my students to find partners. The students in the twosomes have five minutes to interview their partners about one thing they know how to do particularly well, other than writing. After the interviews are done, we form a circle. The participants introduce the people they have interviewed and tell us what they have learned about the subject matter. Quickly, we get a sense of the workshop members as individuals, learn about shared interests, and loosen up. The students tend to feel confident because they have shown an expertise. To follow up, as a take-home assignment, I ask the students to interview a parent or adult relative about an area of expertise. The students bring this information back to class and make oral reports on their findings. This leads to a writing exercise: to use the details of what they've learned—how something is done—in a one-page story. We discuss the benefits of writing a story with specific details. We look at why it's more fun to have a character holding an Allen wrench or an artificial ball-and-socket joint while engaged in dialogue, instead of the perennial cup of coffee. As a side benefit, most of my students are surprised to learn things they didn't know or imagine about their parents or relatives. In a direct, experiential way, the complexity of character is illuminated.

I tell my students: If you have two writers and one has just injured her head, you can be sure that the one dialing 911 is asking, *What was going through your mind as the pipe came toward your skull?* And the reply is: *Do you know if this kind of pipe is used in plumbing or electrical? And if you have a ruler handy, I'd like to get the gauge.*

CAI EMMONS

BRAIDING TIME

Cai Emmons is the author of two novels, *His Mother's Son* and *The Stylist*. Prior to writing fiction she was a dramatist. She currently teaches creative writing at the University of Oregon.

The pleasure of fiction is like the pleasure of snooping—you're in someone else's house when s/he's not looking and you get to poke around in private places that are usually off limits. You find illicit things: racy lingerie, junk food stashes, old journals, court summonses, unsightly photographs, adolescent poetry, sex toys, riveting and sometimes comical evidence of fetishes, addictions, obsessions, sources of satisfaction or shame.

Snooping in fiction takes you even deeper, straight into people's brains and hearts. It takes you to the places which, in our day-to-day lives, we are always guessing about but rarely come to know. In fiction we get to know what characters are *thinking*—not all the time (what a drag that would be!), but when it's important. We get to know what characters are feeling too, again, not moment by moment, but when knowing a character's feeling discloses and clarifies our story's purposes.

It is this open access to human hearts and minds that has always drawn me to the reading and writing of fiction, but to write gracefully about a character's thoughts and feelings is not easy. First there is the challenge of knowing your character well enough to know how she thinks. Is her mind firing rapidly from one thing to another, or does it meander slowly? Does it cycle obsessively around one persistent thought? Does it linger on past events and relationships? Is it stuck in fears or dreams about the future? Has it mastered the art of "being here now"? The following exercise is an opportunity to focus on how your character thinks, focusing in particular on how s/he experiences time. It will help you begin to paint your character's mental landscape.

This exercise is helpful in deepening and authenticating character, exploring in particular how a character *thinks*. It can also be useful in learning to weave exposition deftly into a story.

We all live within a complex weave of three strands of time: the present, the past, and the future. At any given moment our minds are shifting from the focus of the moment to what we anticipate might come next, to incidents from the recent or deep past that still preoccupy us. In the unraveling (or inventing) of a character's relationship to all three elements of time, the writer becomes more deeply acquainted with her character.

EXERCISE

Choose a character to work with, one whom you may already know somewhat but seek to know better. You will write four paragraphs using this central character.

In the first paragraph, your character should be involved in some present ongoing action (preparing a meal, looking for a lost object, going to pick up a date, etc.). The exercise yields more if you give your character a problem or conflict.

Now, keeping the character still engaged in the ongoing activity, write a second paragraph in which the character is imagining something s/he will do (or that will happen) in the future.

In your third paragraph, still using the present activity as a starting point, write about something from the past that the ongoing action is prompting your character to remember.

In your fourth and final paragraph, use elements of forward-looking and backward-looking as your character continues with, or completes, the action. Work on making transitions between time frames feel continuous and smooth.

DIALOGUE

SNOOP 'DA DIALOGUE

Steven Schwartz is the author of two collections of stories, *To Leningrad in Winter* and *Lives of the Fathers*, and two novels, *Therapy* and *A Good Doctor's Son*. His fiction has received the Nelson Algren Award, the Sherwood Anderson Prize, a National Endowment for the Arts Fellowship, and two O. Henry Awards. He teaches creative writing at Colorado State University.

H ere's the secret of dialogue: it's read with the eye, not heard with the ear. You perceive it faster than you hear it. So although spoken dialogue can be provocative, intriguing, and fresh, it can also be wordy, clunky, and vague. The little "ums," "uhs," "you knows," and "likes" slow it down for the reader, as do the redundancies and fillers in actual speech. And whereas real conversation depends on an exchange of information, fictional dialogue has to create character, tension, immediacy, as well as form a compelling design: one long talky paragraph followed by another character's similar monologue just won't cut it.

This is an exercise to help discover the similarities and differences between real speech and fictional dialogue:

EXERCISE

In a public place, and without being noticed, collect fifteen lines of dialogue from at least five different conversations (i.e., no more than three lines from each conversation). Now select ten of your lines and use them to write a coherent, convincing scene. Feel free to add narrative and dialogue you've created to make your scene hang together. Compare the dialogue you've overheard and the dialogue that you've created for your scene. What are the differences in rhythm, characterization, content, specificity, and resonance between the dialogue you collected and that which you made up? Think about why you selected certain lines of dialogue over others. Finally, use your scene—or a piece of it—as a spark for a new story.

DIALOGUE WITHOUT WORDS

Sands Hall is the author of the novel *Catching Heaven*, a Ballantine Reader's Circle selection, and *Tools of the Writer's Craft*, a book of writing essays and exercises. Her produced plays include an adaptation of Louisa May Alcott's *Little Women* and the drama *Fair Use*. She is a graduate of the Iowa Writers' Workshop and holds a second MFA in Acting; her experience as director, actor, and playwright gives her a unique perspective on the writing process. She is an Affiliate Artist with the Foothill Theatre Company in Nevada City, California, and teaches at numerous conferences and workshops, including the University of California, Davis, Extension Programs; the Community of Writers at Squaw Valley; and the Iowa Summer Writing Festival.

My experience as playwright, director, and actor has underscored how often and how clearly characters communicate even when they are not talking to one another. What we might call dialogue also arrives in the form of gesture or movement, in what is not said, in actions that are taken instead of speaking. A great deal of work can be accomplished before (and while) words are spoken by our characters, by carefully selecting the setting in which they are found and the activities in which they are engaged. A reader infers a lot about character from these details. It's also important to know what each character wants, as there is no point to a scene without a strong need of some kind being either accomplished or denied.

EXERCISE

This exercise can at first be frustrating, but students invariably tell me that the exercise shows them how they rely too much on spoken word to communicate the essence of a scene. A typical reaction is: "Because my characters couldn't speak to one another—or, in the form of inner thought, to themselves—I learned a lot not only about dialogue but about 'showing' versus 'telling.'"

For a revealing exercise in writing dialogue, don't use any dialogue.

To begin: It is useful to write a sentence or two describing the tension you intend to explore between your characters: What does each one want?

Reveal character A in a *place* (setting) *doing* something (activity). Character B might already be in the scene, or B might enter. Either way, B has a strong need or want—an ISSUE she wants to address. B interrupts or engages A, who also has an objective—something he is trying to get done, and/or something he does or does not want to talk about. This clash of objectives is an important element in a scene.

Example: Rick is in his study, rigging up a new zip drive to his computer. He needs it because his computer keeps crashing and a major project is overdue. In comes his estranged wife, Miranda, wanting the one hundred dollars he promised would be his share when they went Dutch on a "we-*can*-make-this-work" dinner three months before. But she knows it won't be effective to ask for the money, straight out, so her approach is indirect, nonverbal: she handles his tools, she finds a way to touch him, she sidles around to what it is she really has come to accomplish. . . . All before she begins to speak to him.

Or: we find two people in bed: the décor in the room, the state of the sheets, the actions they perform—opening a window, pulling on boxers or a nightgown, an embrace or touch, or the lack of these—

reveal something about at least one of these characters, and what this moment is for him or her.

Focus on selecting and utilizing setting and activity so that your readers discover—because you show them, rather then tell them—something essential about at least one, if not both, of your characters.

Do not use dialogue. The assignment is to have setting and action, not something your characters say, communicate to the reader. This may be frustrating, and give you all kinds of ideas about what you WILL have them say to each other when you have a chance. Also, do not tell us what they would be saying. Part of the effort is to explore how we communicate without words.

Similarly, avoid "exposition-y" inner thought. Inner monologue can be a method, to be avoided here, of telling rather than showing your reader the content of a scene. A character can think, or reflect, but not in order to convey the tension or her opinions about the tension.

SO: *Using no dialogue,* in less than three hundred words, let the reader discover something about the relationship between two characters by where we find them, what they are doing, and how they interact with each other.

LON OTTO

HEARING VOICES

Lon Otto has published two collections of stories—*A Nest of Hooks*, winner of the Iowa School of Letters Award for Short Fiction, and *Cover Me*. His writing is in *Flash Fiction, Townships, American Fiction*, and *Best Words, Best Order*. Since 1997 he has been teaching courses in fiction technique in the University of Iowa's Summer Writing Festival. He is a professor of English at the University of St. Thomas in St. Paul, Minnesota, where he teaches writing and literature.

Dialogue is one of the most *immediate* elements in fiction. When we hear someone's voice, that person is present for us—here, now. We're in physical contact, and real time and narrative time fall into step with each other. Also, of course, nothing fills a page faster than a column of terse dialogue scrambling down along the left margin, though that's probably not the best motivation for using it. Neither is the desire to convey basic plot information to the reader, which often leads to dialogue that's forced and artificial, characters unnaturally telling each other what they're planning to do, reminding each other what's already happened. Most good dialogue, I think, is driven by the peculiarities of character and situation. The exercise below emphasizes those motivations. It begins with listening—to actual people talking as well as to passages of dialogue from published fiction. Developing a good ear for dialogue sometimes involves attention and verbal acquisitiveness verging on rudeness.

EXERCISE

Preparation

Start listening to how people say things. Develop the habit of eavesdropping on conversations at work, in restaurants, on buses. Quietly write things down that strike you as peculiar or revealing. Read and reread aloud passages of dialogue in stories that seem to you especially effective regarding this aspect of craft. Notice when and how it's used. Look for some of the following characteristics of most effective dialogue:

- Sounds natural—sounds like people talking. This is an illusion achieved largely by relaxing the hold that rules of grammar and syntax have on your writing, and by avoiding complex, gracefully balanced sentence structures.

- Feels motivated by character and situation, rather than seeming contrived to deliver plot information to the reader.

- Reflects setting. The particular environment intrudes in various ways, interrupting, distracting, encouraging or discouraging bluntness, etc.

- Proceeds organically rather than mechanically. It doesn't necessarily follow a logical order (question followed by answer to the question, assertion followed by agreement or disagreement with the assertion), nor does it always stick to the same subject, or make clear transitions from one topic to another.

- Includes gestures and other body language.

- Involves tension of some sort.

- Is particular and surprising.

Writing

Write a new scene in which two of your characters are talking about a third. Create that scene as vividly and naturally as possible using primarily dialogue, with the barest of attributing tags necessary to mark changes of speaker. Don't comment on the *way* things are said. Try to give us a sense of all three distinct characters. Be very clear in your own mind about *where* the conversation is taking place, and consider how that affects what the characters say. Incorporate as many characteristics from the list above as possible.

DIALOGUE EXERCISE: THE NON-APOLOGY

Thomas Fox Averill, an O. Henry Award winner, is the author of two novels, *Secrets of the Tsil Café* and *The Slow Air of Ewan MacPherson*. His work also appears in three short-story collections: *Ordinary Genius, Passes at the Moon,* and *Seeing Mona Naked.* He is writer in residence at Washburn University of Topeka.

As a writer, I am partial to dialogue exercises because I often compose by ear. I hear what characters are saying to themselves and to each other. After I have a sense of voice and interaction, I create scene and dramatic action to accompany what voice and dialogue have inspired me to know about characters and possible plot. My novels, *Secrets of the Tsil Café* and *The Slow Air of Ewan MacPherson,* as well as the stories in my recent collection, *Ordinary Genius,* often use dialogue as a key part of drama, plot, and insight into character and meaning.

Besides its use for inspiration, dialogue is also an effective way to hook a reader into a story, creating an immediate sense of character and conflict. To work well, dialogue needs to contain embedded tension and conflict. Dialogue also needs to suggest what has led to it: its own past, what some writers call "back story."

I've found the apology that is not an apology, what I call the "Non-apology," to be a great way to make sure I and my students start dialogue dramatically. I'm also a believer that fiction often mirrors our lives, at least as a starting point, and I admit to all the non-apologies I've made in my life (my students confess theirs, too).

This dialogue exercise can be practiced individually or in pairs, and works best in a classroom/workshop where everyone can discuss it together.

EXERCISE

Start with the line "I'm sorry, but . . ." and contine with the non-apology, one character to another, getting at as many of the circumstances of the situation as possible.

If you work in pairs, then one writer leads with "I'm sorry, but . . . " and the other responds to whatever it is without advance warning. Say someone writes, "I'm sorry, but I told you yesterday never to talk back to me." The next writer has to define whether this is parent/child, husband/wife, boyfriend/girlfriend, teacher/student, or some other possibility. The writers have to define, too, what happened when the one talked back. Each writer responds to the other, and together they create a story in dialogue.

Once writers have written for fifteen minutes or so, these pieces need to be read aloud. They often contain similarities in the writers' strategies: buried anger, counteraccusations, demands for apologies for other things, cold distance, and working things out. These dialogues also tend to mirror good dialogue practice: to always heighten, re-define, and surprise yourself and the reader.

I would suggest reading some good dialogue before beginning. Two poems are good. William Carlos Williams begins his "This Is Just to Say" by confessing that he's eaten plums from the icebox. His non-apology comes in the last lines, when he notes, "They were . . . so sweet and so cold." Kenneth Fearing's "Love, 20¢ the First Quarter Mile" begins with apology, for lying, for making "pronouncements a bit too sweeping," for damning his lover's extravagance and maligning her tastes, and slandering "a few of your friends."

But he continues with forgiveness, with his obsession for his lover, and with the realization that, should she accept his apology and return, then everything is likely to happen all over again. Once teachers and students know the exercise, other examples will present themselves.

LEVELS OF DIALOGUE

Douglas Unger is the author of four novels, including *Leaving the Land*, a finalist for the Pulitzer Prize and winner of the Society of Midland Authors Award. His most recent books are *Voices from Silence* and a collection of short fiction, *Looking for War and Other Stories*. He is the co-founder of the MFA in Creative Writing International Program at the University of Nevada, Las Vegas, and serves on the executive board of the International Institute of Modern Letters (IIML), a supporting organization for the literary arts around the world.

Dialogue in life is most often a transaction—a bartering of desires and intentions implied under the surface of literal communication. In fiction, language in dialogue should be hyper-refined, made far more intense than everyday speech. As my friend Jim Heynen puts it, "The part of a story where a fiction writer should most feel that s/he is doing the work of a poet is not in description or narration but in dialogue." As the late great Raymond Carver used to say, "Good dialogue is angled toward a character's intentions."

After years of teaching and writing with different dialogue techniques, I've broken them down into four categories, keeping in mind that there are no set rules, and that many wonderful stories vary and combine all types of dialogue in lively scenes.

The first category is "open dialogue," composed of flat, rhetorically empty lines, such as lines spoken in meeting and greeting, similar to an "open scene" in acting classes. Then there is "informational dialogue" or "first-level" dialogue, which communicates facts, directions, plot information, and is used mainly for the initial setup of stories. "Dialogue by omission" or what I call "second-level" dialogue relies on the technique of leaving portions of speeches unstated and crucial parts of sentences incomplete, to be filled in by the reader's imagination. And "third-level" or "dialogue of opposition" is a final category, which inverts or works against the literal meaning of the language in the spoken lines with respect to the characters' intentions. The quicker a story can get to "second-level" or "third-level" dialogue, the more engaging it is to our imaginations.

EXERCISE

Second-Level Dialogue

1. Write a scene that plays on the familiar trope of the girl telling the boy that she's pregnant, in which A is a girlfriend and B is a boyfriend. Imply that B is happily expecting the news, but that A, unhappily, feels compelled to admit that the child may not be B's after all. Don't let either character mention pregnancy. Let each character guess at the next statement of the other and finish each other's lines.

2. Create a dialogue about gift giving, in which A is a parent and B is a child. On the table is a wrapped gift. B expects the box contains a pocketknife he's been asking for, while A is pleased she's picked out the expensive fountain pen she always desired as a gift when she was B's age. Write the scene through to the unwrapping of the gift without either

character mentioning a pocketknife or a fountain pen. Try variations on this scene with gifts of your own choosing: sneakers instead of trendy running shoes, a deep-sea fishing reel instead of a fly reel, widely different books, etc.

3. Prisoner A is let out of a cell by B—who is either a captor or a warden—and is then led down a dark hallway. A believes this is a final journey to execution. B lets A go on believing this for a while. Before getting to the end of the hall, B lets it be known that A is going to be set free. Keep the scene going until the door at the end of the hallway is opened. Don't let either character speak of death or execution, and don't let either mention freedom.

In writing these exercises, shape the speeches so that characters pick up on half-stated lines or complete each other's thoughts. Try one character "stepping on" or cutting off another character's lines. Find at least one moment in which what a character means to say is best expressed by not speaking. Experiment with different devices on the page to indicate silence.

For masterful examples of second-level scenes, study the conversation between the governess and Mrs. Grose near the close of chapter 21 in *The Turn of the Screw* by Henry James; and the tender love scene between Valentin and Molina, in chapter 14 of *The Kiss of the Spider Woman* by Manuel Puig. Much of Puig's erotic scene is wordless, stimulated by pauses indicated by an ellipsis, "— . . . ". Silences and pauses are techniques of second-level dialogue.

Third-Level Dialogue

The point of each exercise is to work the scene toward characters stating lines either exactly the opposite to or at an extreme angle toward what they really intend, for example, the way someone might comment ironically about a stormy day, "What a great day for a picnic"; or when a driver intends an apology to a passenger he just picked up and got stuck in a traffic jam, "Looks like we're taking the scenic route." An excellent literary example is how Ernest Hemingway closes his novel *The Sun Also Rises* with Jake's third-level line, "Wouldn't it be pretty to think so?" Or study Hemingway's "Hills like White Elephants" and the way the girl says she feels "fine" when she feels terrible, and uses the word "happy" ironically. Third-level dialogue is also angled toward misunderstandings, or how characters—as many people do in life—often don't listen very well to what the other person is saying.

1. Two friends, A and B, are walking far out in the country. They are overtaken by unexpected extreme weather— heavy rain, intense heat, an ice storm, etc. It was A's idea to take the walk in the first place. B is out of sorts about this and complains to A about what B is suffering in statements expressing to A exactly the opposite of what B feels and observes.

2. A and B are enthusiastic lovers. While making love, they play a game of describing to each other their intense pleasure by turning around what they are really feeling and stating just the opposite.

3. Write a scene in which a young soldier, A, has just returned from a war. B is the soldier's lover and can't help but urge A to talk about war. A responds to B's questions only at an extreme angle, with the language of music, the language of sports, the language of foreign travel, language drawn from books.

PLOT AND PACING

FICTIONAL BUILDING BLOCKS

Dan Chaon is a National Book Award Finalist for his short-story collection *Among the Missing*, which was also cited as one of the Notable Books by *The New York Times*, *The Washington Post*, and *Publishers Weekly.* He is also the author of the short-story collection *Fitting Ends* and the novel *You Remind Me of Me.* He teaches at Oberlin College.

Frequently, we think of stories in terms of plot and movement—beginning, middle and end, rising action and resolution, and this is a very useful model. At the same time, stories are not merely two-dimensional triangles, and I like the way that the brilliant Canadian writer Alice Munro describes her short fiction, as a house with various rooms that one can wander in and out of, not necessarily in any prescribed order. There have been times when it's been useful to think of short stories in this way, as a kind of house, made up of a variety of "rooms" and other "architectural" features which serve a variety of functions, practical and aesthetic. Below I've listed some of the basic building units that I think of as I'm working on a piece of short fiction.

EXERCISE

For this exercise, you will write several sections of a short story. Each section should be no longer than two to three paragraphs. You can organize these seven sections in any way you want.

A: Write a section which introduces some conflict, need, or tension into the life of your character. This section could be as short as one sentence. Its purpose is to create some sort of suspense or forward-movement in the story.

B: Write a section which describes the setting of the story. Setting, to my mind, doesn't mean simply landscape or location. Rather, it's a broader term which refers to the fact that stories happen, at some level, in a particular location, time, and moment—possibly including the sociology of the world of the characters, the details of socioeconomic position, the age, race, class, gender, etc., of the character, and most especially the way the character is or is not aware of these as factors in his life. A story should exist in a place which the narrator/character has some relationship with.

C: Write a section which describes the texture of the character's day-to-day life—a sense of a palpable, clearly definable present which exists in relation to a past and a (presumed) future. What does the character do all day long? What are her habits and pleasures? The writer ought to give a sense that the character exists in a definable present, which exists in relation to a past and a future. The past and future need not be clearly mapped out (though often they are necessary) but they should exist in a story, if only as a sort of meta-awareness. Quite simply: You are here. Once you were there. Someday you will be someplace else.

D. Write a section which develops the character as a presence, using some dialogue and balancing it with description and summary. Think about different ways that people are characterized in fiction—physical description, gesture, background history, dialogue, thoughts and actions, what others say about the character, even his name.

E. Write a section which dramatizes some aspect of the world that the character fears, some sense of doubt or dread. It may be that the character's notions of the world are incorrect. She may never get what she wants. There may be some other version of life that is far more interesting, vital, and true than the path he has chosen. Every bad thing that your character imagines exists in the world, and is in wait.

F. Write a section which evokes a particular resonant image that is important to the character. Don't explain why the image is important or what it means—just describe it vividly.

G. Write a section, using dramatized scene and avoiding summary, which shows the character engaged in some significant action. When you're done writing all these sections, you may have the skeleton of a story. Or you might not. In any case, these are some of the elements that I think of as I'm writing a story, and I thought it might be helpful to you to break a story into fragments as a way of thinking about what elements are important to you as a writer. Are there any elements here that you would leave out? Are there any "pieces" that you would add?

KEEP THE ENGINE RUNNING

Renée Manfredi is an associate professor of English at the University of Alaska in Fairbanks, where she teaches creative writing at both the undergraduate and graduate levels. Her collection of short stories, *Where Love Leaves Us*, won the Iowa Short Fiction Award. She is also the author of two novels, *Above the Thunder* and *Running Away with Frannie*. She is the past recipient of a fellowship from the National Endowment for the Arts, a Pushcart Prize, and a regional winner in *Granta* magazine's Best American Novelists under 40 competition.

Pacing seems to be a problem for many beginning fiction writers. They have trouble getting their characters to do things—writers are a contemplative lot and their characters tend to reflect that. Occasionally in my writing classes I'll get some speed freaks—young writers who in the space of a seven- or eight-page story deal with divorce, infidelity, substance abuse, and a car crash or two—but mostly when there's a problem with pacing, it's a problem of inertia.

Here, then, is an exercise I wrote for a student whose character would not get out of a swimming pool for eleven pages. I've used it in subsequent writing classes with good results.

EXERCISE

In this exercise, your job is to put two characters, of any gender, age, or relation to each other—husband and wife, mother and son, pregnant woman and midwife—in a car or truck and send them out for a specific task. This may be an errand, a quick trip to the grocery store, a drive around the neighborhood to look for a lost dog, a trip to a craft store to buy glass eyes for a teddy bear (see pregnant woman, above), a hardware store for dimmer switches, etc.

Here are the rules:

1. The driver of the vehicle will never turn the engine off.

2. They must stop a minimum of FIVE times during this journey—to use the bathroom, to buy a soft drink, gasoline, to check the air pressure in a tire, whatever—and EACH time they stop, they must interact with at least one other person. Note: Not all of the five will, or should, be given equal space in the story. You might find that person #3, for instance, takes most of the narrative time and energy, and the others become lesser values.

3. They will not reach their destination.

4. The entire story will take place in and around the vehicle.

How do the five people the characters meet along the way add to or detract from their journey? Do your primary characters behave differently toward each other after the day's influence of these other people?

The purpose of this exercise is to get your story moving and to show you how the trigger of a story is very seldom the *actual* story.

FRED LEEBRON

THE RIFF

Fred Leebron, program director of the MFA in Creative Writing at Queens University of Charlotte in North Carolina, is a professor of English at Gettysburg College in Pennsylvania, and a former director of the Fine Arts Work Center in Provincetown, Massachusetts. His novels include *In the Middle of All This, Out West*, and *Six Figures*, the film version of which recently premiered at the Toronto Film Festival. He has received a Pushcart Prize, a Michener Award, a Stegner Fellowship, and an O. Henry Award. He is coeditor of *Postmodern American Fiction: A Norton Anthology* and coauthor of *Creating Fiction: A Writer's Companion*.

Eleven years ago, I was working with a film actor on a novel he was trying to finish, and I was struck by how skeletal the book seemed, despite its urgency and unquestionably complex emotion. The book captured quite successfully an imbalanced love affair between an actor and a singer, and kept me reading as I watched the actor's rage evolve.

It was obvious the book was short, but it was quite tight and credible. The question was how to make it more substantial without undermining its focus and its astonishing energy.

I came up with the idea that the writer should attempt to write in another fabric to the story beyond the actor-singer love affair. I suggested that the writer take more time to evoke the actor's complex relationship to his own mother, and I recommended that he attempt this through "riffs" in the voice that would allow the actor to go off on something apparently inessential to the main story line.

The writer did a wonderful job pursuing this strategy, and the book nearly doubled in length and grew even more artfully complex, as he pursued other elements of characters in the same riff style.

EXERCISE

Writing in the voice of a story that you are drafting, allow that voice to go off on something absolutely tangential to the story line. For instance, if you are writing a love story, allow one of the characters (through either third-person interior or first-person interior) to "go off" on how much he or she loves or hates his or her job. Or have him or her remember the first time his or her father took him or her out for ice cream. The purpose here is to inhabit the character fully and to write in a relaxed and lucid fashion, because, of course, this won't become a part of the story because it is tangential to the story line. And then, who knows? Once it is written, you might find a place for it after all.

The term comes from the musical term, especially in relation to jazz, of the riff that goes off from the main notes, from the song itself, and thereby widens and deepens the music.

STORYBOARD YOUR STORY

Brent Spencer is the author of *The Lost Son*, a novel, and *Are We Not Men?*, a collection of short fiction chosen by the editors of the *Village Voice Literary Supplement* as one of the best books of 1996. He is the recipient of a Wallace Stegner Fellowship from Stanford, where he was also a Jones Lecturer in Creative Writing, and the James Michener Award. His short fiction has appeared in *The Atlantic Monthly, GQ, The American Literary Review, Epoch, The Missouri Review, McSweeney's Online*, and elsewhere. He teaches creative writing at Creighton University in Omaha.

One of the hardest things about writing fiction is to get a sense of the whole. Writers need a way to stand back from their stories in order to recognize and address the story's dimension, direction, and development. It's hard to recognize a story's problems when the writer's gaze is locked on words, on dialogue, on figures of speech, or on any of the other aspects of fiction writing. This exercise helps you see your story in a whole new way.

Filmmakers often storyboard a screenplay before it goes into production. A storyboard is like a comic strip, a set of drawings that indicate the key moments of each scene. For the fiction writer, storyboarding can provide an overview that's sometimes lacking.

EXERCISE

Try storyboarding your plot. Reduce your story to a three- or four-panel cartoon strip. Each panel should depict a key action, a turning point, or a moment of change in the story. Impossible? Maybe. Your story may be too complex to be reduced like this. But try it anyway. Even an unsuccessful attempt can help you discover your story's core, which can help you understand how to revise your story.

For example, how would you storyboard *Little Red Riding Hood*?

The first panel might show Red's mother asking her to take the goodies to Grandma.

The second might show her conversation with the wolf in the woods.

The third might show the wolf getting to Grandma's house before Red.

The fourth might show Red at "Grandma's" bedside, about to be eaten (or eaten, depending on the version).

The fifth might show the woodsman saving the day.

Your choices might be a little different, but you can see that the core of the story—its spine—is more visible because of storyboarding. And notice, too, that even a fairly simple story like this one seems to require five panels, not three or four. Or can you reduce it to four without dropping any of the story's key moments?

A short story is more complex than a fable, of course. But the technique can help you find your story's problems. The story with too many scenes becomes an endless string of panels. The story that's little more than an extended conversation becomes a storyboard in which nothing more than a pair of talking heads appears inside each panel.

To test out ideas for development, and to make sure your story's middle scenes are not interchangeable, cut your panels apart and physically rearrange them. Is the story pretty much the same? Then you have a problem. Notice that the *Little Red Riding Hood* panels can't be rearranged without harming the story.

Storyboarding can help you discover whether you have too much story or too little. It may reveal that your story's ending is really your beginning or that one character (or more!) has no real impact on the core of the story and can be cut. It might show that the sequence of events isn't as tightly constructed as it should be.

Storyboarding helps you see your story as more than a collection of words, but as a depiction of characters, their actions, and the consequences of those actions. It's also a lot of fun.

SEAN MURPHY AND TANIA CASSELLE

STICKING TO THE STRUCTURE

Sean Murphy's novel *The Hope Valley Hubcap King* won the Hemingway Award for a First Novel and was featured on the Book Sense 76 list for 2003. He is also the author of *The Finished Man*, *The Time of New Weather*, and *One Bird, One Stone*. Tania Casselle is a freelance writer. Her fiction has appeared in the short-story anthology *Harlot Red* and journals including *South Dakota Review*, *Carve* magazine, and *The Bitter Oleander*. Murphy and Casselle teach creative-writing workshops both privately and for academic and arts organizations.

W e find a consistent challenge for many of our students, both in fiction and creative nonfiction, is finding the narrative structure that best works for the story they are trying to tell. Here is a two-part exercise that works the "muscles" of structural development in a way that may open up new possibilities.

EXERCISE

Part 1: Narrative Development
Handle this as you would a free-writing exercise, with the additional dimension of a constantly expanding subject. Write for two

minutes on each prompt (use a timer), remember to keep your hand moving forward, no editing. Flow directly from each prompt to the next, without stopping. Ideas may arise that you don't consciously perceive yet. You can try writing each prompt several times, taking a different angle each time. Don't be deceived by the term "story." This does not just apply to fiction—it applies to any narrative form, whether it's fiction, memoir, creative nonfiction, or even reportage.

- Tell us where your story begins.

- Tell us what everything depends on (in your story).

- Describe the moment it all changes.

- Tell us what complicates things.

- Tell us where it all ends.

- What does everybody want (in your story)?

- What does everybody fear (in your story)?

Part 2: Narrative Arc/Structure and Flow

This part is especially for those who are struggling to "organize" their narrative, whether it's fiction or nonfiction. Perhaps you have lots of free-writes, tons of material, notes and scenes, etc., and are trying to order it all to get a balance of direct action, reflection, digression, back story, introducing characters, reported summary, facts to include, or whatever. Perhaps you want help with keeping the story or plot moving forward, keeping the pace going with continual variation, without having too many pages of reflection at once, or otherwise interrupting the main action in a way that slows things down? Perhaps you're not sure if you're stringing the order together in a way that serves to build the narrative arc?

So, take a normal-size block of Post-it notes. On separate squares, write down each specific scene/incident that you know has to go into the manuscript, or specific lines of thought you want to explore, bits of back story, a flashback or flashforward, a description, a fact, or whatever. Just jot down a few words of summary to remind you what you're referring to. Use just one Post-it note for each aspect. Break it down as much as possible. You might have a long piece of reflection that is currently twenty pages, but if you think about it, it actually covers three different areas, so you could put each one on a separate Post-it note. Give yourself maybe fifteen minutes to jot down the *main* contents, without getting too hung up on every single thing you could put in. The simple act of setting a time limit will show you something—the ones you come up with are probably the *most important* elements to include in your manuscript.

Then, experiment with putting them in order. You'll probably know what has to go at the beginning and what has to go at the end. Then jigsaw it all together. Insert things in terms of where they would naturally fit in the story line, looking at a balance of show/ tell, direct action/reflection, and dramatic scenes that move the story forward versus back story. Experiment, keeping an open mind and an attitude of not being attached to the results.

Because they're Post-it notes you can keep playing with your structure—it's fluid. Stick them on your wall. One of our students stuck her lineup on the bathroom wall so she can contemplate them several times a day as she's brushing her teeth. Add in new Post-its as you think of other things; move them around.

Have fun with it! It's an easy and visual way to order the unfolding of your narrative. There won't necessarily be *one* right way to tell your story—there may be a number of equally good but different ways. But this will help you play around with the range of possibilities until you find the one that feels best to you.

WHAT AM I WRITING ABOUT? CLARIFYING STORY IDEAS THROUGH SUMMARY

Kirby Gann is the author of the novels *Our Napoleon in Rags* and *The Barbarian Parade*, and is coeditor (with Kristin Herbert) of the award-winning anthology *A Fine Excess: Contemporary Literature at Play*. He is an editor at the independent press Sarabande Books and teaches in the brief-residency MFA in Writing Program at Spalding University in Louisville.

My writing process is not very time-efficient, but it's the only way that I've learned that keeps my interest going: I plan very little, and uncover or invent the story as I'm writing it. Starting with some vague idea—a situation, a character trait, a sentence that stimulates me—my first draft proceeds by free association, discovery, and, eventually (hopefully), momentum. I try to operate under the notion that the writing should take control of me, rather than the other way around. This can make first drafts very slow going. More important, however, it can make aspects of revision difficult, when the time comes to take control of the material and form it into a story that makes sense to a reader.

A problem I run into often is the inability to formulate exactly what I am writing about, and it can take several drafts before I begin to feel that I know what I'm doing. It is only then that I can decide what the story requires and what in my original draft isn't necessary.

An exercise that helps me in this process—one I don't employ until the second or third draft—is to use summaries of the story events in order to clarify for myself what I'm working toward. Think of the concrete summaries found in those Cliff's Notes guides to classics that you may have used in high school.

In terms of writing a novel, this summarizing is a many-tiered process: start with the general, then move to particulars. A "general" summary might begin, "This is a story about . . ." Try to summarize your novel or short story in a sentence or two. For example, Shakespeare's play *Othello* might be summarized as follows: "This is a story about the soldier Othello, who becomes so mired in jealousy that he ultimately turns into his own victim." If you were writing *Othello*, your recognition of this basic narrative line would greatly help you hone your ideas of how to dramatize that story.

Next, move to particulars: with a novel, you might begin to summarize each chapter (again, in a sentence or two); with a short story, individual scenes. This can help you decide where to open the story: How would one decide to dramatize Othello's jealousy problem? Well, the logical place to begin might be to show how jealousy gets started. Thus the play begins with Iago and Roderigo discussing recent events—most important, Othello and Desdemona's elopement. Roderigo has his own interests in Desdemona, and Iago was supposed to be keeping him abreast of her attachments, and the two must decide upon what is to be done now, etc.

EXERCISE

Write short summaries of whatever story you are working on, preferably keeping the summary within a few sentences. The objective: to make clear to yourself exactly what happens in the story, and, eventually, why and how. Summarizing in this way can work on many levels; once you can describe to yourself the story in a nutshell, you can ask whether or not that story is one that would interest you as a reader; if it's not, summarize it again, perhaps inventing a new twist. Summarize ten different ways, changing the basic story line slightly from one version to the next.

Once you've come up with a summary that sounds like a great story to your own ear, you have a very general outline to keep you focused, and extraneous scenes suddenly become clear (and scenes that need to exist start to appear). Start breaking the narrative into its components and summarize those, keeping in mind that you know now where the narrative needs to go. In this way you can learn what scene needs to occur when.

DOUGLAS BAUER

THE RICHNESS OF
RESONANCE

Douglas Bauer is a novelist and journalist who received his doctorate in English from the University of Albany. He is the author of
Prairie City, Iowa, a nonfiction portrait of the town where he was
raised. He is also the author of three novels—*Dexterity, The Very
Air*, and *The Book of Famous Iowans*—and most recently *The Stuff
of Fiction*, a collection of essays on the craft of fiction writing. He
is the editor of *Prime Times: Writers on Their Favorite TV Shows*.
Bauer is also a former editor of *Playboy* magazine and a freelance
journalist whose articles, essays, and criticism have appeared in
*Esquire, Harper's, Sports Illustrated, The New York Times Magazine,
The Atlantic Monthly*, and *The New York Times Book Review*. He
lives in Boston with his wife and stepson.

I f we keep in mind that fiction worth writing and reading finds
its moments of high drama not so much in a close depiction of
the events that produce them but in the effect of those moments
on the characters they touch, then we have the chance to give our
stories and novels the power literature needs.

EXERCISE

To better understand where and how to locate the points of drama in your stories, start with an incident of high narrative impact: say, a murder, as in Alice Munro's story "Fits," or a bloody brawl, as in Alice McDemott's novel *That Night*. Or anything else you wish to use—a calamitous fire, a violent argument, a fatal accident.

First, to establish in your consciousness the moment you've chosen, write it as a scene of direct dramatic action through the eyes of a character participating in it, using a first-person point of view. The murderer. A combatant in the eye of the brawl. Someone trapped in her apartment as the flames rage outside her door.

The event is now clear in your own mind. Next, using an omniscient narration, revisit it and give readers five to ten physical details of it without mentioning what is centrally occurring. If it's a murder, devote the narrative's attention to the look of the room or the alley or wherever it's taking place. If it's a gang fight, direct the narrative eye to the sky overhead and the broken watch on someone's wrist and the sounds of police sirens in the near distance, et cetera. The idea here is to acquire a sense of how to delay and reroute the narrative on its way to describing the dramatic event itself.

Now, imagine a friend or a lover of the character you created in the first stage of this exercise. The murderer's brother, for example, or the combatant's wife. Or the fire victim's mother. With a year having passed, have the relaxed character speak fully about the incident to a stranger in a diner. Here, you'll want and need to decide why the affected person would decide to talk about the event with someone he or she has never seen before. What's his or her state of mind, or life circumstances, that would initiate the conversation? What about the stranger, the diner, the locals, would cause your character to be reminded of what happened a year ago.

It's this third and final statement that will yield the valid scene, the one that dramatizes the lasting effect of the original event.

SETTING AND DESCRIPTION

MARGOT LIVESEY

SETTING IN FICTION

Margot Livesey was born and grew up on the edge of the Scottish Highlands. After receiving a BA in literature and philosophy from the University of York in England, she spent most of her twenties in Toronto writing and waitressing. Subsequently she moved to the United States, where she has taught in a number of colleges and universities, including Williams College, the Warren Wilson MFA program, and the Iowa Writers' Workshop. She is a recipient of grants from the National Endowment for the Arts and the Guggenheim Foundation and is the author of a collection of stories and five novels, including *Criminals, Eva Moves the Furniture*, and most recently *Banishing Verona*. She now lives primarily in Boston.

In his wonderful biography, *Les Mots,* Jean-Paul Sartre describes how as a boy writing stories, he would bring his hero and heroine to some dramatic point, say one of them had fallen overboard from a small boat, and then spend the next two pages copying out the encyclopedia description of sharks. Of course this makes us smile but it also captures something of the attitude that many of us bring to setting and description. We create our characters with care, we work hard at our plots, we ponder our themes.

Setting, on the other hand, tends to be either a given, or an afterthought. It's rare to read a review that says, "Great setting," and in workshops and critiques, readers often take the setting for granted.

175

But in the stories we most admire setting is absolutely integral: the characters could only exist in that particular world. Moreover setting offers a rare opportunity to the writer to make her or his work new—particularly useful in dealing with family relationships—and to allow characters to be more active. So rather than setting a mother/daughter story in the kitchen where the two women are yet again chopping vegetables and stirring sauces why not have them repair a bicycle or groom a dog or prune an apple tree? Rather than setting the story of two brothers in a bar where they're forced to alternate between smoking, drinking, and arguing, set them to building a rock garden or stocking an aquarium.

Perhaps this will involve some research, which is one of the great pleasures of fiction writing. You can focus on setting both as a useful tool for revision or as a way to nudge forward your current work. Is the setting helping the story as much as it could? Might a more interesting setting allow you to deepen the characters?

Whether you decide to change the setting or to stay with the one you've already created, the next task is to see whether your prose in those parts of the story can work at a higher level. Often as writers we reserve our best prose for those parts of the story that we think matter most, and it's always worth looking at our descriptions to see if we can come up with better details and more interesting syntax.

JIM HEYNEN

THE CHARACTER OF SETTING

Best known for his short-short stories about "the boys," Jim Heynen has published widely as a writer of poems, novels, nonfiction, and short fiction. His stories about the boys have been featured often on National Public Radio's *All Things Considered*, as well as on radio in both Sweden and Denmark. Minnesota astronaut George "Pinky" Nelson took a taped collection of the stories for bedtime listening on his last space mission. The most recent collection of these stories, *The Boys' House*, was named an Editors' Choice for Best Books of 2001 by *The Bloomsbury Review*, *Newsday*, and *Booklist*. He is currently writer in residence at St. Olaf College in Northfield, Minnesota.

L et's try to create an atmosphere through description of the world around the character.

EXERCISE

Think of one long paragraph. Introduce the character in the first sentence, and then describe the setting. Return to the character only at the end of the paragraph.

The idea is to create atmosphere and tone through setting description that will affect how the reader sees the character and understands her/his situation—or how the character regards her/his own situation.

For example:

Elaine knew that this time her mother's illness was not hypochondria. She walked toward the river and along the path where the melting snow provided the best, the cleanest, walking. The bare branches were alive with birds whose songs were crisper now without the muffling leaves of midsummer or the chilling silence of winter. The vireo, the wrens, the brazen blue jays all appeared like bright vocal ornaments on the sharp-edged branches. Last week's ice was gone from the river and it moved in its quickened spring pace, dark with spring runoff but still lustrous under the April sun. Ferns were breaking through the crusted layers of last year's fallen leaves, like green fingers curled into fists and just starting to open as if in a handshake to the warm sun. Elaine knew this spring was going to be cruel, that for her it was going to be a season of unwanted beginnings.

Consider all options. Maybe the character's situation stands in contrast to the setting. Maybe it is dictated by it. The setting itself could be an exact description of a room, a town, or even an item of clothing that dominates the atmosphere of the scene. Writers like Joseph Conrad have, of course, given us some precedents for setting with a personality of its own, but feel free to experiment with possibilities.

JOAN LEEGANT

ANIMATING THE INANIMATE

Joan Leegant is the author of a collection of stories, *An Hour in Paradise*, which won the L. L. Winship/PEN New England Book Award and the Edward Lewis Wallant Award for Jewish Fiction, and was a finalist for the 2004 National Jewish Book Award. The book was also a fall 2003 selection in the Barnes & Noble Discover Great New Writers Program. Leegant is a recipient of an artist grant from the Massachusetts Cultural Council and several fellowships at the MacDowell Colony in New Hampshire. Formerly a practicing attorney, she teaches writing at Harvard.

Ascribing feelings and behaviors to inanimate objects can add surprising elements to your fiction. In one of my own stories, for example, a character carries around a raincoat, which at one point slides off his lap "as if it didn't want to be there." This ascribing of emotion to the raincoat allowed me to heighten the character's awkwardness through an unusual point of view—that of his raincoat—which doesn't want to be there in the room with him. Similarly, in another story, the zero on a digital clock glares at a character who is lying on the telephone. This allowed me to show the character's torment over the phone call through an unusual source: the accusing clock which presumably knows he's not telling the truth.

But ascribing feelings and behaviors to inanimate objects does more than simply illuminate character; it can also add depth and texture to the world of the story by suggesting that all things—

living and otherwise—play a role in our lives, even if we are not aware of it.

EXERCISE

The next time a physical object appears in a story of yours that seems to have significance for the action or the character— windshield wipers working hard on a rainy night, a pair of shoes hiding in the back of the closet, a vacuum cleaner that stubbornly breaks every time your character attempts to use it—try giving that object some emotions or behaviors of its own, and see what it does for your characters and story. Allow yourself to be as tentative or as full-throttle about the object's feelings and behaviors as you like, and be open to what it can show you about the world of your story.

VENISE BERRY

LEARNING TO LAYER

Venise Berry is the author of three national best-selling novels, *So Good, An African American Love Story, All of Me: A Voluptuous Tale*, and *Colored Sugar Water*. In 2003 she was honored with the Creative Contribution to Literature Award from the Zora Neale Hurston Society. *All of Me* received a 2001 Honor Book Award from the Black Caucus of the American Library Association. Her two most recent nonfiction projects are *The Historical Dictionary of African American Cinema* and *The 50 Most Influential Black Films*, both coauthored with S. Torriano Berry. She is at work on a new novel and a work of nonfiction. She is an associate professor of journalism and mass communication at the University of Iowa in Iowa City.

I n my opinion, good writing is not a talent that you must be born with, but a talent that you can learn. Here is a simple layering exercise that can help you to become a good writer—a very good writer.

EXERCISE

In a first draft, your goal should be to simply get the information out of your head and onto the paper. So you should sit down at your computer and start typing. Don't worry about every little detail at first. Once the story is down on paper that is when you begin to use layers to develop it.

For example, in the first draft you might write:

She walked into the room.

All you need in the first draft is to get the character into the room. Now add a layer to improve the sentence and give your reader more information.

She slowly walked into the darkened room afraid of what was waiting for her inside.

This second version tells us a lot more. Now add another layer.

After grabbing her husband's gun from the closet, Constance slowly walked into the darkened room afraid of what was waiting for her inside.

With the information about the husband's gun and by giving her a name, we have heightened the suspense. Now add another layer by using more specific words in certain places.

After grabbing her husband's small silver pistol from the hall closet, Constance slowly limped up the stairs and into the darkened bedroom afraid of what was waiting for her inside.

This layer of details gives the reader an even more powerful picture of what is going on. Changing general words like *gun* to *small silver pistol* or *walked* to *limped* helps us get a better understanding of the circumstances. Clarifying places like *hall* closet, *up the stairs* and *bed*room helps us picture the action more clearly.

Finally, we can add a layer of background information by letting our reader know what is going on in her head.

*After grabbing her husband's small silver pistol from the hall
closet, Constance slowly limped up the stairs and into the darkened bedroom afraid of what was waiting for her inside. Despite
his constant abuse, an overwhelming sadness suddenly filled her
soul—fourteen years of marriage were over.*

Going into her head at this moment helps us to understand not
only what she is about to do, but why.

Using this layering technique shows you how easy it is to turn
five simple words into a powerful paragraph that tells us so much
more.

PATRICIA POWELL

A SENSE OF PLACE

Patricia Powell is the author of *Me Dying Trial*, *A Small Gathering of Bones*, and *The Pagoda*. She is a visiting writer in the graduate program at the University of Houston.

I use this exercise frequently in my beginning fiction class in order to get students to think about setting. So often when they write, students don't have a specific place in mind. As a result, their stories feel a bit disembodied. There are no details to ground the reader or the characters. It's impossible to see where the characters are and to be able to locate them in place and time. We can't see or hear or smell anything. The story becomes confusing and unfocused.

This exercise is also a way to get students to think about details and physical sensations; it's basically a tour through the five senses, a guided visualization. I did not make up this exercise, and I can't remember now where I found it. But I use it quite a bit and I've changed it around some.

EXERCISE

Close your eyes and go back to a place where you used to live. It may be in a different town or country. It doesn't matter. See yourself walking toward the house or building, and begin to take into account everything you see: the shape of a house, the limbs of a tree, scrawny dogs, bloated cows, kids on the street, the games they play. Pay attention to the winding road, the muddy footpaths, the color of the sky, box-shaped buildings, the light on the horizon.

Then take a deep breath, and begin to recount everything you smell: smoke, cow patties, stagnant water, freshly mowed lawns, baking bread, tires burning, rubbish burning, exhaust, blood, dust, damp, mildew, paint.

What do you hear? Children at play, roosters crowing, dogs barking, traffic on the roadway, a heated argument, someone playing the piano, the shrieking cicadas at night, someone singing, someone shouting?

And what do you taste? What particular meals were prepared here, food items you get only when you return to this place: tamarinds, guava, barbecued ribs, curry goat stew?

Last, bring your consciousness to your belly. What do you feel as you step inside that house and go through room after room, listening to sounds and allowing yourself to be awash in memories?

Now open your eyes and, without thinking about plot or perfect sentences, pick up your pen and everything that comes to mind, *write now.*

During this exercise, students often go back to a house or a town or a particular country that has a lot of emotional resonance. What's most interesting is that the moment they close their eyes, they hook immediately into this setting. And this is great, because now that they have a place that's very familiar to them, a place where the characters can pretty much relax and come alive, now they can get on with the business of writing the actual story. Oftentimes the setting doesn't bring back good, happy memories, but these complex feelings only help to create a very emotionally charged sense of place.

BE THE TREE

John Smolens's recent novels include *Cold*, *The Invisible World*, and *Fire Point*. He is a professor of English at Northern Michigan University.

Fiction is full of objects—clothes, cars, trees, houses, lockets—and good writers select the stuff that occupies their fictional worlds with great care. An object that is integral to a story has to have purpose and singularity—as much, really, as any character in the story. There have been times when I've brought objects to my workshops, or have asked participants to do so; we sit around these objects—a meerschaum pipe, a necklace, a rusty gardening trowel—and write about them, treating them as though we were artists working on a still-life painting.

However, one of the most successful exercises has been when I artificially limit everyone's access to the objects. This I prefer to do outdoors, on a day when the weather is fair (often a challenge here in northern Michigan). The participants had been asked to bring a handkerchief or bandana to the session. We then go out to a small stand of woods and I break the group up into pairs; one partner blindfolds the other, and then I lead them through the woods and silently direct the seeing partner to help the blindfolded partner to touch a tree—its bark, the leaves, roots, etc. And then we move on to an outcropping of granite, or some puddles. The roles are reversed so that everyone has the opportunity to spend several minutes experiencing the physical world without the sense of sight.

Then we go back inside and I ask the group to write about the objects they just experienced while blindfolded. The results are often remarkable: it's clear that the other four senses—touch, sound, taste, and smell—compensate for the lack of sight, and they often write about these objects in the natural world from the *inside*. One writer who wrote a very good piece about a pine tree explained to us that she felt she had become the only tree left standing on earth.

An exercise such as this works best in an unfamiliar environment, preferably out-of-doors, weather permitting. But perhaps there are also other places in school or on campus where the students could convene.

EXERCISE

Write a five-hundred-word descriptive passage that does *not* employ any visual details, but does offer sensory detail based on taste, touch, smell, and sound.

GEOFFREY BECKER

A VERY, VERY LONG SENTENCE

Geoffrey Becker is the author of *Bluestown*, a novel, and *Dangerous Men*, a collection of short stories that won the Drue Heinz Literature Prize. Most recently, his stories have appeared in *Ploughshares, The Antioch Review, Prairie Schooner* and *The Best American Short Stories* 2000. He teaches fiction writing at Towson University in Baltimore.

EXERCISE

Think of a place you know well—your hometown, or perhaps some other neighborhood in which you once lived. Now, think of that place on a Friday night. For thirteen full minutes, write about it, using lots of specific detail to bring the place to life. Feel free to do anything you want—you can write in third person, first, or a combination. You can follow a bug up a lamppost or explore the thoughts of a kid stealing Slim Jims from a convenience store. There is just one rule: *You may not end the sentence* (no cheating with semicolons, either!). When the thirteen minutes are up, everyone reads aloud. (While I usually do this with groups, it can certainly be done solo, as well.)

Why I do this:

A lot of fiction writers are scared to death of poetry, of singing publicly, and of losing control. Short, declarative sentences are easier to construct, they tend to stand their ground in a solid way, and they often win the approbation of high school English teachers. This exercise stretches a completely different set of writing muscles, forcing the writer to make associative leaps—the kid stealing the Slim Jim looks out the window and sees a passing truck with a dog in the back, one of its ears standing straight up like the hood of the '53 Chevy in the junkyard over on Elm, where raccoons snuffle behind the battered metal trashcans—that he might not have ordinarily made, just to keep the thing going. While the results from this exercise more often resemble prose poems than what we usually think of as fiction, for many students the experience of taking such a deep breath, of attempting to extend syntax to the near-ridiculous, can open up hitherto untapped veins of poetic sensibility that will be useful for future attempts at more conventional storytelling. Plus, it's fun.

I like timed exercises; they take the burden off the writer. You write for thirteen minutes, and there you go—whatever you wrote, that's what you've got. It's not that good, you say? Of *course* it's not that good—I only gave you thirteen minutes. If I'd given you thirteen hours, you'd have come up with a masterpiece. If it's not any good, that's *my* fault. I've had writers in classes whose stories—the ones they labored over and submitted for workshop—were tense, stilted, and unimaginative, but who, when doing this exercise, suddenly wrote like completely different people. Why that happens is mysterious, but I suspect it's a combination of having an assignment, and of surrendering control and allowing one's subconscious to do the driving. I once heard Eddie Van Halen say that for him, playing a guitar solo is like falling down a flight of stairs and landing on his feet. I think this exercise is a little like that, just with a really long flight of stairs.

I recommend reading García Márquez's "The Last Voyage of the Ghost Ship," for a good example of a one-sentence short story that's poetic, funny, and spooky all at once.

KAREN E. BENDER

MOST MEMORABLE FOOD: USING SENSORY DETAIL

Karen E. Bender is the author of the novel *Like Normal People*, which was a Washington Post Best Book of the Year and a Barnes & Noble Discovery Book for 2000. Her short fiction has appeared in *The New Yorker, Granta, Zoetrope: All-Story, Ploughshares, The Harvard Review, Story,* and other magazines, and has been reprinted in *The Best American Short Stories* and *The Pushcart Prize* anthologies. Her stories "Eternal Love" and "The Fourth Prussian Dynasty" were read by Joanne Woodward and Frances Sternhagen, respectively, as part of the *Selected Shorts* program on NPR. She has received grants from the Rona Jaffe Foundation and the National Endowment for the Arts, teaches fiction writing at the University of North Carolina at Wilmington, and is working on a new novel and collection of stories.

I believe that you need three elements to become a good fiction writer: honesty, craft, and patience.

Here's why you need each one:

As people, we live in our own separate worlds. How does one ever know what it is really like to be another person? Honest writing is one way to look into someone else's mind, to get a glimpse of what it is to be another human. When you write honestly, you create a bridge to another person.

Learning a craft is a way to give your honesty a form. Mastering elements of fiction, learning about all the different ways writers have used techniques such as dialogue, plot, sensory detail, etc., will help you find the best way for you to express your feelings and evoke a similar emotion in the reader.

Finally, patience will help you produce work better than you ever imagined you could. Staying with a project, seeing it through revision after revision, taking the time to allow it to evolve, will make it better.

EXERCISE

Using sensory detail is one way that you, as a writer, can learn to really perceive the world in your own way. What does the light look like at dawn? How do red traffic lights reflect in the wet street after a rain? How does a city smell in the summer versus the winter?

Now take a chocolate chip cookie, or a potato chip, or some familiar food item that you have not really looked at before. Examine the food in all of its sensory elements. How would you describe this food to someone who has never seen it before?

Look at, smell, touch, examine the cookie or chip and then eat it. Take ten minutes to write about the food, describing it as specifically and with as much sensory detail as you can.

Next, write two pages describing a memorable or important food in your life. It can be a single item of food, like a Snickers bar, or it can be an entire Thanksgiving dinner. It can be a food that you love or hate, as long as it is memorable.

Describe the food so the reader can clearly see/smell/hear/ taste it. Some questions to think about: Is it in a package? How does it look on a plate? Do you eat it with your hands, knife/fork, or what? How does it sound when you chew it? What surrounds this food? Are you the only one eating this food? Do you eat it at a particular time—when you're happy, joyful, etc.? What are other people around you doing? Are you in a coffee shop, at a dinner table, beach, carnival? Are people around you eating a food that you wish you had? Do you feel superior/inferior eating this food?

One alternative to this exercise: Go outside and describe the environment around you. Then describe a place that has been important to you.

BRET ANTHONY JOHNSTON

LIKE WATER FOR WORDS:
A SIMILE EXERCISE

Bret Anthony Johnston's first book is *Corpus Christi: Stories*. His work has appeared in such publications as *The Paris Review, Prize Stories: The O. Henry Awards 2002*, and *New Stories from the South 2003, 2004*, and *2005*. His novel *In The Minor Keys* is forthcoming from Random House, as is a writing exercise anthology that he is editing. Bret Anthony Johnston teaches writing at Harvard University.

One of the first exercises I give writers in my fiction workshops is to page through whatever anthology we're reading that term and read the first line of every story. We usually use an anthology containing fifty or so stories, and as the students are reading the opening lines, I ask them to make a list of their five favorites. The goal is to consider how the particular language, the unique combination of punctuation marks and letters, makes us want to read while the other lines fail to excite us in the same way. Finally, of course, we want to figure out how the authors do it so that we can pull readers into our own stories, seduce them with our own commas and nouns.

If Amy Bloom's wonderful story "Silver Water" is in the anthology, I can expect upward of half the class to choose her first line as one of their favorites: "My sister's voice was like mountain water in a silver pitcher; the clear, blue beauty of it cools you and lifts you up beyond your heat, beyond your body."

Some students will choose the line simply because they also have a sister, often a sister who seems as mysterious and powerful as the narrator's; others will be lured in by the subtle and dark "was" that so masterfully hints at the loss that is the story's engine, and still others will come to the story for the sheer pleasure of reading such lyrical language, a desire to spend time in the presence of such a lovely voice. Obviously, I can relate to all of these—what sensitive reader couldn't?—but of the hundreds of times that I've read the story, what always draws me in is this single, common word: Like.

A lesser writer—or by extension, a less affecting narrator—would have compared the sister's voice to music (maybe a sad, haunting Wagner piece), to the hiss of winter wind through the branches, to a sound! But not Bloom, not her precocious narrator, Violet. The genius here is using the simile to broaden, rather than narrow, the reader's understanding and experiencing of the story. By comparing a voice (that is, a sound) with something other than a sound (that is, anything except something auditorily received), the author assures the reader that her characters view their lives through unexpected and exceptional lenses; the implicit agreement with the readers is that by the story's end, they too will see the world differently. What more can we ask of literature? What more do we hope to offer our readers? It's a lesson we can all take to heart, a tool we should all have in our toolbox.

THE OBJECTIVE

To avoid clichés in our similes by engaging the senses in unexpected, original ways.

EXERCISE

Complete the following similes and strive for specific details and tight, lyrical language in your comparisons. Take your cues from Amy Bloom, and try to resist the temptation of comparing a sound with a sound, a taste with a taste, a scent with a scent.

— The morning sun tastes like:

— Her voice smelled like:

— The music sounded heavy as:

— The color green feels like:

— The color red tastes like:

— Midnight rain is bitter as:

— The wind looks as _____ as:

— Seeing him walk was like hearing:

— Tasting the night's dinner was like watching:

— Hearing her cry was like tasting:

— Smelling the gasoline was like touching:

— Touching her dying father's hand was like seeing:

Of course, my hope is that one of the similes you come up with will fit into a project you're currently working on, or that it will spark an idea for a new and exciting piece of work. On the most practical level, however, the goal is to simply exercise your imagination and condition your writing mind to aspire toward surprising and compelling ways to use language.

One way that I've used this exercise, both as a writer and a teacher, is as a set of linguistic calisthenics that I do before beginning the day's "real" work. Give yourself five or ten minutes to write through the prompts—or write through prompts of your own—and exclude everything from your mind except the twenty-six letters of the alphabet and their infinite combinations. Focus on the language. See the world through your characters' eyes rather than your own. Let the ink sing like a violin, let the letters smell like a lover's hair, let the words pour like silver water.

CRAFT

FINDING A LARGER TRUTH BY TURNING AUTOBIOGRAPHY INTO FICTION

Susan Vreeland, two-time winner of the San Diego Book Awards' highest honor, the Theodore Geisel Award, writes fiction on art-related themes. Her works include *Life Studies*, a *Los Angeles Times* best-seller; *Girl in Hyacinth Blue*, a *New York Times* best-seller and Book Sense Book of the Year Finalist, and a Hallmark Hall of Fame film titled *Brush with Fate*; *The Passion of Artemisia*, a *New York Times* best-seller and a Book Sense #1 Pick, and for which Vreeland was named Author of the Year, 2003, by Hatchard's Booksellers, H.R.H. The Prince of Wales, England; and *The Forest Lover*. Her novels have been translated into twenty-fve languages.

Many new writers begin with autobiographical material. Beware. An exacting adherence to truth rarely makes good fiction. Good fiction still must have these basic elements: believable, sympathetic, and complex characters; intense yearning; obstacles to fulfillment of this desire (i.e., conflict; best if an outer one suggests an inner one); a concrete setting in time and place; a narrative arc (in simple terms, an inciting event, working through the conflict, arriving at some sort of resolution). Mere recording of lives rarely provides this.

You can escape the tyranny of fact and produce something larger and deeper by doing this exercise.

EXERCISE

Step One

Take two events that happened at slightly different times in your life. Write two or three pages on each, separately. It could be mostly narrative summary. You will put it into scene with direct dialogue later, unless the dialogue comes easily on this first draft. Suggest what growth or character change occurred as a result of each.

Step Two

Think about how these events would have been impacted if they happened simultaneously. If the moods are different, would the character vacillate between them? Would one dominate over the other? Would one experience make the other experience happen differently? Would the main character learn something different, grow or change in a different way because of the two events occurring together? Most likely, yes, if you've picked well. Work toward creating an entirely new dynamic requiring new exploration and invention beyond the mere recording of memory that you did in step one. Write a narrative summary of the new story.

Step Three

Add to the character based on one important element you don't have, and take away one element that you do have. Such elements might be: personality characteristics; attitudes; social or regional background; nationality; level of education; ability, interest or passion. These can't just be tacked on your existing material. They must reshape it.

Step Four

Search deeply for those issues in which the truest self of this *new person* resides. Now write your fiction with scenes and dialogue accordingly.

Step Five

Check your results with the basic elements of fiction listed in paragraph one.

For guidance, you might wish to read my autobiographically based story, "Crayon, 1955," in *Life Studies,* which is the result of following these steps.

SHEILA KOHLER

SECRETS OF THE GREAT SCENE

Sheila Kohler is the author of five novels: *The Perfect Place, The House on R Street, Cracks, Children of Pithiviers,* and *Crossways;* and three collections of short stories: *Miracles in America, One Girl,* and *Stories from Another World.* She has taught creative writing at Bennington College, City College in New York City, the Chenango Valley Conference at Colgate University, Sarah Lawrence College, The New School in New York, the State University of New York at Purchase, the West Side YMCA in New York City, and in Montolieu, France.

When we think back to our first and perhaps most lasting impressions of literature what comes to mind is often a moment from a fairy tale. We may think of the moment when the merchant sees the radish in the witch's garden and plucks it, only to be confronted by the witch herself who demands in return the creature who will greet the merchant first on his return home. Or we relive the moment when Sleeping Beauty, wandering alone through the dusty attics of the palace, comes across the spindle, only to prick her finger and fall into the deepest of sleeps; or the moment when the prince calls out, "Rapunzel, Rapunzel," who lets down her hair only to find, not the witch, but the prince, who climbs up the high tower and into her arms.

Later we may recall scenes from our favorite novels: Jane Eyre, in the novel of that name, perhaps, locked up in the bedroom where her uncle has died, and seeing what she takes for her uncle's ghost. Or Pip in *Great Expectations* wandering with the ancient Miss Havisham among the remains of her wedding feast under the stopped clock; or Rodolphe's seduction of Emma during the agricultural fair in *Madame Bovary*. All these vivid and indelible moments come to us in scenes.

Why do we remember them? What is it that makes them indelible in our minds? What are the elements that render them unforgettable? And, if we ourselves wish to create something that will transport our readers and remain with them forever, how do we go about it? What are the elements in the Great Scene? And what are the scenes we need for the story we wish to tell?

THE BASIC ELEMENTS OF A GREAT SCENE

I would suggest, very simply, that like the princesses in the fairy tale, these elements might be grouped into three categories:

1. Place: the witch's garden, sunlit with the radish shining temptingly; or the dusty attic where the dangerous spindle lurks; the tall tower where the witch has confined Rapunzel; or the red room with its mirror, its four-poster bed, and its deep red hangings; Miss Havisham's wedding feast spread out on the table with its cobwebs and mice running in the rotting food; or the contrasts between the manure and the mundane cows and the terrace above, where Rodolphe woos Emma in Flaubert's contrapuntal and ironic scene of seduction at the agricultural fair.

2. People: the adventurous, reckless merchant/father; the young vulnerable princess; the lovesick prince; Jane, the poor orphan girl; Pip, the poor lower-class boy; Emma,

the bored provincial woman looking for passion—all
people who lack something; are looking for something,
people desirous of something; people thwarted in some
way by an adversary: the witch; the wicked fairy; Jane's
selfish relatives; Emma's seducer, Rodolphe; or rescued or
helped by a savior: the prince.

3. Plot: Something happens in these great scenes, something
    that changes the lives of these people in some way; a stone
    is thrown into the water which will ripple: plucking of the
    radish will mean the giving up of the daughter who greets
    the merchant on his return; she will be relinquished to the
    witch; the fit Jane has in the bedroom will mean the arrival
    of Mr. Brocklehurst and Jane's banishment to boarding
    school; Rodolphe's seduction of Emma will ultimately
    bring about her downfall and her death.

EXERCISE

This exercise gives us the opportunity to practice the art of writing
an unforgettable scene, bearing in mind these elements and the fact
that talent, as Maupassant says, comes from originality: an original
way of perceiving, understanding and judging the world.

1. When describing a place, use a place you know well with
    familiar, original, but significant objects, which may suggest
    what is up ahead: the radish, the spindle, the mirror, the
    manure, the rotting food.

2. People. Use original people from your own lives, those you
    know well or those you have observed from afar and
    dreamed about; people who need something or think they
    need something or want like Oedipus to find something out.

3. Plot: Remember that plot comes from the characters: it is from the characters' wanting that comes jeopardy of some unexpected kind or, on the contrary, salvation or epiphany which may be granted to them.

Students are asked to write these three parts of a scene separately and then to combine them.

TONY ARDIZZONE

HEMINGWAY'S CAROMS: DESCRIPTIVE SHOWING AND TELLING

Tony Ardizzone is the author of six books of fiction, most recently the novel *In the Garden of Papa Santuzzu*, and the collections *Taking It Home: Stories from the Neighborhood* and *Larabi's Ox: Stories of Morocco*. He is the editor of the anthology *The Habit of Art: Best Stories from the Indiana University Fiction Workshop*. His work has received the Flannery O'Connor Award for Short Fiction, the Milkweed National Fiction Prize, the Friends of Literature's Chicago Foundation for Literature Award for Fiction, the Pushcart Prize, two National Endowment for the Arts Fellowships, and other honors. He teaches in the creative-writing program at Indiana University.

I encourage the writers with whom I work to read widely, and to understand that each work they encounter offers them an opportunity to learn something new about craft. This involves their ability to read as a writer, with an eye on technique, on the specific ways a particular effect in a given work is achieved. In the same way that apprentice painters learn and refine their craft by first identifying and then imitating the techniques of their masters, so writers can develop their craft by looking more closely at works they admire, identifying aspects of the works' techniques, and then imitating those aspects. Here is an exercise based on these principles.

In a letter to a fellow writer, Ernest Hemingway wrote the following about his method of description: "I always try to do the thing by three cushion shots rather than by words or direct statements." To put this into context, "three cushion shots" is a term used in a game called three cushion billiards, which is played on a table with no pockets and with two white cue balls and a single red ball, called a carambola. The object of three cushion billiards is for each player to strike both the opponent's cue ball and the carambola, but before doing so bounce off three or more cushions (or make three caroms, a word derived from "carambola") before both balls have been hit. Doing so scores a point and allows the player to continue.

What Hemingway was suggesting to his friend was that the best description more often than not is indirect. Rather than aim directly at a specific aspect or attribute of character (e.g. honesty, intelligence, attractiveness), the skillful writer often relies on series of caroms, or indirect statements, to suggest or show the character traits the writer intends to reveal. Direct statements about character are overt and *tell* the reader about the character. Descriptive caroms are specific and suggestive and *show* the reader intended character traits, and by doing so involve the reader more closely in the experience of the character and the fiction. This is the concept behind the creative-writing teacher's suggestion to "Show, don't tell."

EXERCISE

Look at examples of description in the fiction you read and identify the direct statements and the caroms that the writer uses as well as the character traits that these indirect descriptions suggest. Then choose one of the examples as a model and write a description of one or more characters (a woman, a man, a boy, a girl), relying on caroms of your own.

HOW TO OWN A STORY

Robert Boswell is the author of *Century's Son*, *American Owned Love*, *Living to Be 100*, *Mystery Ride*, *The Geography of Desire*, *Dancing in the Movies*, and *Crooked Hearts*. He has received two National Endowment for the Arts Fellowships, a Guggenheim Fellowship, and numerous prizes for his fiction. His stories appear in *Esquire*, *The New Yorker*, *The Best American Short Stories*, *The O. Henry Prize Stories*, *The Pushcart Prize* anthology, and in many literary magazines. He teaches at New Mexico State University, the University of Houston, and in the Warren Wilson MFA Program. He resides with his wife, Antonya Nelson, and their two children in Texas, New Mexico, and Colorado.

EXERCISE

1. Find a story that speaks powerfully to you, but one that you have not really studied.

2. Photocopy it and reread it.

3. Read it again and underline the sentences that have something special to them—extra resonance or especially effective expression.

4. Read it again and circle the imagery that recurs in the story. (Mark also any special lines that you missed before.)

5. Read it again and highlight the spots where a character's motivation is suggested or revealed. (Some lines may be underlined *and* highlighted.)

6. Read it again and ☐block out☐ the places where key character-actions take place.

7. Go back to the book and photocopy the story again.

8. . Read it again and physically draw boxes around the sections of the story—boxing up the scenes and the narrative passages that more or less stand alone. Box the scenes in one color ink and the narrative passages in another color.

9. Read the first section and divide it up into beginning, middle, and end by boxing them off and labeling them. What determines the beginning, middle, and end? Think about them in terms of shape. The beginning suggests a shape, the middle forces a turn or expansion or compression that gives life to the shape, and the end shows or suggests the ramification of the beginning or middle.

10. Reread the first section and read the second section before dividing the second section into beginning, middle, and end, boxing and labeling as before. Do the same for all of the sections of the story, going back each time to the beginning and rereading before moving forward.

11. Read the story again and underline the key sentences that make the story move forward within the individual sections and double score the lines that force movement among the sections. That is, underline the sentences that push a scene from its beginning to its end and double underline the ones that do that on the larger scale of the story (that don't just push forward the scene but push forward the whole momentum of the story).

12. Make a chart of the story's sections (scenes and narrative passages) and number them. On the same chart, further divide each section into its three parts (beginning, middle, and end). Then divide the whole story into its three parts (beginning, middle, and end); each part may hold several sections.

13. On the chart, beneath each part of each section, write out all of the sentences and images that you've previously marked. Add any other things that seem important, such as elements of craft that you've noted, details of setting that serve a larger purpose, suggestions of theme, recurrent motifs, etc.

14. Read the story again.

This exercise will teach you how to shape a scene and how to shape a story.

OBJECT LESSONS

Elizabeth Searle is the author of three books of fiction: *Celebrities in Disgrace*, *A Four-Sided Bed*, and *My Body to You*, and winner of the Iowa Short Fiction Prize. Her stories have appeared in *Redbook*, *Ploughshares*, *AGNI*, *Ontario Review*, *Michigan Quarterly Review*, and *The Kenyon Review*, and in the anthology *Lovers*. She has been cited three times in *The Best American Short Stories* and twice in *The Pushcart Prize* anthology, and has won the 2000 Lawrence Foundation Prize for Fiction. She has taught writing in the Bennington MFA and the University of Southern Maine's Stonecoast MFA programs. She is the vice chair of PEN/New England and runs the annual Erotic PEN readings. She lives with her husband and son in Massachusetts.

I came up with this exercise after an "object lesson" of my own, one that helped me pull together the title story of my first collection, *My Body to You*. While struggling through draft after draft, I found myself always including a "charged" detail—one that interested me, though I didn't know why.

In my case, a whippet dog from my childhood showed up in key scenes with no clear purpose. So I decided to systematically break it down: What about that dog so interested me? To find out, I free-associated on the dog.

First, I realized that the body of the whippet—greyhound-like, only smaller—reminded me of a Barbie Doll body: hourglass shaped and all "hard," no soft flesh. Writing this description made me realize why my main character was fasting, why she was so distracted by jiggling flesh on her subway ride. Her body had been violated and, to her, the whippet dog represented a longed-for freedom and invulnerability.

I also remembered, while free-associating, a story about another dog. A friend of mine from high school had run away from her violent sister, taking along only her dog. This memory led me to create a scene where my heroine escapes her own violent home taking with her the whippet, who struggles in her arms and wounds her, triggering other key plot events.

Finally, while concocting metaphors for my whippet, I found myself comparing the dog—who always seemed poised to run—with an airplane that is poised for flight. This gave me a final image for my story. My heroine sits in a plane: about to fly off and marry, for safety, her gay best friend. She is reminded of her old whippet by the other planes awaiting takeoff; this causes her to reflect in the last line that what she's about to do (take off; marry her gay friend) may be "a perfectly natural act."

After I finished the story, I realized that analyzing this whippet had helped me create several scenes and had given my story an overarching, recurring metaphor: a lot of mileage gained from one "object." Since then, my students who have tried this exercise have reported similar clarifications and mini-breakthroughs.

I always tell students to search their own drafts, as if with a divining rod, for "sources of energy," especially those objects or concrete details that seem particularly—sometimes inexplicably—interesting. Such charged objects can teach us valuable "lessons" about our stories.

EXERCISE

1. List three or more concrete details from your story draft that seem to you especially interesting or potentially

"charged" with metaphoric possibilities (or simply details that you feel belong in the story and you are not sure why).

2. Think about each detail and write several paragraphs on each one; these writings may evolve into scenes or descriptions or may help you in a more general way as you seek to enrich and deepen your story.

Consider, as appropriate, the following:

- Describe the detail thoroughly; including any changes it's undergone. Use metaphors liberally in your description.

- Describe how the detail came into your characters' lives, including any little stories or incidents associated with it.

- Describe what, if anything, your character does with the object (any secret major or minor rituals) and what memories or associations the object has for your character.

- "Free-associate" on the detail/object, letting it trigger memories or remanding from your own life (anything goes).

THE GOLDILOCKS METHOD

Rosellen Brown is the author of ten books, five of them novels: *Half a Heart, Before and After, Civil Wars, Tender Mercies,* and *The Autobiography of My Mother;* three collections of poetry: *Cora Fry, Cora Fry's Pillow Book,* and *Some Deaths in the Delta and Other Poems;* a collection of short stories: *Street Games;* and a miscellany of poetry, essays, and fiction: *A Rosellen Brown Reader.* Her stories have appeared numerous times in *The Best American Short Stories, The O. Henry Prize Stories,* and *The Pushcart Prize* anthology, and one of them was included in *The Best American Stories of the Century,* edited by John Updike. She is the recipient of the Award in Literature from the American Academy and Institute of Arts and Letters, an Ingram Merrill Foundation Grant, the Janet Kafka Award, a John Simon Guggenheim Foundation Fellowship, National Endowment for the Arts Grants, and a Bunting Institute Fellowship. She teaches in the MFA in Writing Program at the School of the Art Institute of Chicago.

This won't sound very sexy, or even much like an exercise, but it's by far the most important thing I have learned to keep in mind when I write: You should begin your story once and then again and yet again, changing point of view and a whole lot more, radically if you can. Do not accept your initial opening gambit. And don't look at your earlier openings. Start fresh. You could call it the Goldilocks Method.

EXERCISE

I have sometimes brought my work sheets to classes to prove that I'm not exaggerating when I tell my students that some of my most satisfying stories have started so unpromisingly, so boringly, that they would be humiliating to show anyone but a class of working writers. But here's the thing: All (well, almost all) your work should be done well before the first page is finished. By the end of the first paragraph, in fact, or in revision, you ought to have asked yourself half a dozen crucial questions:

- Who will tell the story? The most obvious point of view is not always the one that gives you the best vantage point on the action or the characters, or guarantees the greatest narrative intensity. If you have begun your initial draft in the first person, make it third person, which is not just a question of changing "I" to "he" or "she" but rethinking your narrator's distance from the characters or situation. If you are using the first person, how close to the action is the narrator? How much does he or she know? Is the best teller of that tale the character to whom something happens or perhaps someone slightly removed? Might it be one or many onlookers who are not deeply implicated at all, like the town that speaks in a communal voice in Faulkner's "A Rose for Emily"?

- If you have started in the past tense, try the present: Do you need a sense of immediacy or the reflective quality of retrospect? Are we hearing things as they happen (impossible, of course, but "as if," a convention we accept), or is this a reconstruction? If so, is it in the simple past or is it a distant recollection, a haunting memory, many years old?

- Are you beginning at the right moment—not, say, in the mind of a character waking up or driving to where a confrontation will take place, which is a kind of stalling, but right smack in the deep waters of the encounter?

- Do you want to begin with a large summary statement—"It wasn't beautiful but he loved his life"—or *in medias res*— "The baby is in her carriage for the first time"—or maybe even in the middle of a conversation?

- Can you get a really different bead on your characters by putting them in a radically off-center situation? For example, in my story "Questionnaire to Determine Eligibility for Heaven," I literally kill off my narrator and have her fill out an application, by the end of which, after justifying the way she has lived her life, she ends by scolding whichever heavenly judge is presumably reading it for not sharing her passion for justice.

- What is the narrator's tone or attitude toward the proceedings? Earnest? Arch? Pained? Angry? (And so forth.)

- And what kind of language best represents that tone— colloquial, formal, transparent, flamboyant?

- Find an anthology or a book of stories by a writer who interests you and specifically study opening lines and paragraphs: other people's stories and novels are your best teachers.

As you contemplate the variety of their writing, you will understand why you should never accept your default setting: compress a situation into a sentence, expand it with a dozen petty details, do a close-up, pan from a distance, turn it into a letter sent or unsent, a suicide note, the description of a photograph or a set of instructions (see examples as diverse as Jonathan Swift's "Directions to Servants" and Lorrie Moore's wonderful collection *Self-Help*). Bend it, twist it, play with it. Treat your story like a malleable piece of clay whose shape is not a given. First thought is not necessarily best thought; in fact, it rarely is.

For a fascinating nonfiction example of what can happen when you invite such variations, find Janet Malcolm's *New Yorker* profile of the painter David Salle called "Forty-one False Starts" (in the magazine's archives or in David Remnick's anthology, *Life Stories*). There you will confront a multiplicity of ways to approach a single character, in this case a real, not a fictional, one. Clearly, Malcolm could not decide on the best way to capture her subject. I suggest you purposely invite such inconclusiveness. It's slow and it feels inefficient but you might find your most richly realized story hidden where you least expect it.

SANDRA SCOFIELD

BIG SCENES

Sandra Scofield is the author of seven novels, including the National Book Award finalist *Beyond Deserving*. Her most recent book is a memoir, *Occasions of Sin*. Her craft book for writers, *The Scene Book*, from which these exercises were adapted, will be published by Penguin in 2007.

I have noted, over and over, that apprentice writers express a fear of "big scenes." They are comfortable with two or three people in the room, but suggest to them that a story really needs a little more commotion, and they seize up. "How will I handle all that action?" they ask. "How do you plan when so much is going on?"

The simple answer is, the same way you plan any other scene. By thinking of:

A: the function or purpose of the scene—why have it, and why have it here?

B: the pulse of the scene, or the source of its energy

C: the shape of the scene, that is, its structure, and

D: of course! the actions and emotions of the scene.

The best way to prepare to write such scenes, which, by the way, are lots of fun, is to read such scenes with a writer's eye. Here are two reading exercises to help you understand how Big Scenes are constructed. Keep in mind that "beats" are small units of action in a scene that move the scene along both in terms of what is happening and emotionally.

EXERCISE

1. Reading Big Scenes for Beats

Read a big scene several times until you feel you have the flow of it and can hold it in your mind. Then study its elements. Identify the focus in the scene: What does it keep coming back to? A topic of conversation or disagreement? A person? An event in the past or one that is about to happen? State this focus.

Take the scene apart by listing the beats of action. Now go over those beats and star or underline those that are the most important, that form the heart of the scene, that are related to the focal issue or person. What, then, is the effect of the other beats? Do they simply make it possible for the core actions to happen, or do they amplify them in some way? Identify the point where there is either confrontation (and something gets resolved) or a clear avoidance of it that ends with unresolved conflict that will carry over into another scene.

Consider how the nature of the event itself and the environment contribute to the flow of beats and the movement of the dramatic action.

This is a lot of work! You might begin by looking at a scene and concentrating on only one element of analysis, then coming back and adding another, or possibly moving on to another scene and considering two elements this time, and so on.

The best examples will be those you have enjoyed and admired. All in all, big scenes are challenging. If you feel put off, that's fine. Maybe later, maybe never. Maybe you'll think like the creative-writing instructor in Alice Munro's story "Differently" who tells a character about her writing: "Too many things. Too many things go-ing on at the same time; also too many people. Think, he told her. What is the important thing? What do you want us to pay attention to? Think."

2. Big Scene Dossier

Spend some time imagining circumstances and characters that might combine in a suitable setting to make a big scene. List as many kinds of settings, circumstances and events as you can think of where people could gather.

Select one at a time and think of a conflict that might arise out of the event or situation itself (such as a fight in a bar). Then think of a conflict that might arise in such a situation that would have nothing to do with the situation or event itself, but could get played out there. (Family and friends confronting a "user" at a birthday party where he is spoiling the fun. Or an unexpected pregnancy being re-vealed at a business conference. And so on.)

The idea is simply to stretch your mind around the possibilities. Keep adding to your list. The less obvious the connections are, the more fun your scenes will be. Watch real life, of course, for ideas!

MOVING THROUGH TIME: A FOUR-PARAGRAPH SHORT SHORT

Nancy Reisman is the author of the novel *The First Desire* and the story collection *House Fires*, which won the Iowa Short Fiction Award. Her fiction has appeared in several journals and anthologies, including *The O. Henry Prize Stories 2005, The Best American Short Stories 2001, Bestial Noise: The Tin House Fiction Reader, The Kenyon Review, Glimmer Train*, and *Michigan Quarterly Review*. She's received fellowships from the National Endowment for the Arts, the Wisconsin Institute for Creative Writing, and the Fine Arts Work Center in Provincetown, Massachusetts. For the past several years she's taught graduate and undergraduate fiction workshops at the University of Michigan and the University of Florida, and she now teaches at Vanderbilt University.

Fiction writing seems to me haunted by small and larger questions about time: how to navigate through time, how to represent the time-sense of experience, how emotional intensity, states of consciousness, memory, and time-sense relate. One nuts-and-bolts way emerging writers can approach these questions is in working with the movement between scene and/or image—which involves immediacy, intensity, and a relatively slow experience of time—and summary, which allows quick travel at a greater distance. I think emerging writers benefit from mixing these elements, experimenting with different combinations, and tracing their effects.

One of the beauties of short shorts is that their brevity allows writers to conceptualize the whole, and immediately see how the play of time affects a piece and the experience of reading it.

The poet and fiction writer Ron Wallace asks his students to write "One-Page Novels" and the notion of a one-page novel gets at crucial issues with larger applications. How does one quickly cover a significant sweep of time and information while offering enough immediacy and intensity to deeply engage readers?

Inspired by Ron Wallace, I developed a formula for a short short that covers a long time span. I offer a four-paragraph formula as a starting point, and encourage writers to stretch it, alter it, lengthen it, break it apart, reshuffle elements—to reinvent it for themselves. In the most successful of the resulting short shorts, the "formula" becomes a buried substructure.

EXERCISE

I designed the exercise for adult writers—the youngest writers to whom I've offered this exercise have been in their late teens—but it can be adjusted. The Four-Paragraph Formula is as follows:

1. Paragraph 1: Focus on a moment from childhood, and render that moment with precise sensory detail. I recommend using moments from before or up to the age of twelve.

2. Paragraph 2: Begin with a phrase like "For the next decade . . ." which will push the writing toward summary.

3. Paragraph 3: Begin with a line of dialogue, and move into scene. This brings the focus back to an immediate moment and increases the intensity.

4. Paragraph 4: Begin with a phrase like "After that, and in the following weeks . . ." which will again push the piece toward summary and the larger view.

One of the gifts of this exercise is that it encourages new writers to befriend temporal prepositions/prepositional phrases. I think of prepositions as great unsung heroes of language: they are essential to all kinds of navigation, to moving through time and space and defining relationship.

The short short operates on its own terms, but it can also serve both as a small-scale model—literal and/or conceptual—for moves writers often make in longer stories and novels, and as a point of comparison for other ways of navigating. As a writer, I've been interested in portraying characters' interior lives and states of consciousness, and I've worked with longer time spans: I am often looking for ways to juxtapose a moment and a larger life. The underlying concept here—of defining precise points, their larger contexts, and ways to move between them—comes into play through many aspects of fiction-writing.

JOY PASSANANTE

USING THE RETROSPECTIVE LENS

Joy Passanante is the associate director of Creative Writing at the University of Idaho. Her poems, essays, and stories have appeared in numerous magazines including *The Gettysburg Review, Short Story, College English,* and *Alaska Quarterly Review.* She has won several awards for fiction, poetry, and script writing, including two fellowships and a grant from the Idaho Commission on the Arts. She is the author of three books: *Sinning in Italy, My Mother's Lovers,* and *The Art of Absence.* Her fiction has been a finalist for the Ben Franklin Award, the Idaho Book of the Year Awards, and the ForeWord Magazine Awards for 2002 and 2004.

This exercise allows the writer to pull together several elements of and techniques for writing fiction as well as non-fiction—particularly, setting, atmosphere, dialogue, characterization, and even research.

EXERCISE

1. Imagine your parents in a single significant watershed moment in their lives before you were born. This moment might be their first meeting, first date, first kiss, or a moment when they experienced a conflict or made a major

decision (e.g., buying a house, having children, getting divorced, eloping).

2. Dramatize that moment in two one-to-two-page scenes, one from each parent's point of view. Use the first person in both scenes. To develop these scenes, you will use dialogue, setting, and atmosphere.

3. Note that you may need to do some research to develop the scenes fully and complexly. What is the date of this significant moment? What did people wear then? What were the idioms that were popular or otherwise characteristic of this period? You might want to examine old photographs so that you can use details of appearance to flesh out your characters. Or you might want to interview your parents (e-mail or phone will work, of course). Where were they during this moment? Inside? (What were the interior décor characteristics of houses and buildings then?) Outside? (What were they looking at?) How might the setting and atmosphere look and feel different to each parent?

This exercise can help you leap into a full-fledged story or personal essay.

AMY BLOOM

WATER BUDDIES

Amy Bloom is the author of a novel, *Love Invents Us*, and two collections of stories: *Come to Me*, which was nominated for a National Book Award, and *A Blind Man Can See How Much I Love You*, a nominee for the National Book Critics Circle Award. Her stories have appeared in *The Best American Short Stories*, *The O. Henry Prize Stories*, and numerous anthologies. She has written for *The New Yorker*, *The New York Times Magazine*, *The Atlantic Monthly*, *Vogue*, *Slate*, and *Salon*, and has won a National Magazine Award. *Normal: Transsexual CEOs, Crossdressing Cops, and Hermaphrodites with Attitude* is her first book of nonfiction and explores gender varieties. Bloom teaches at Yale and lives in Connecticut.

EXERCISE

An approach to workshops and an exercise that can also be done by writing friends working as a pair, or fellow writers who meet in a class or writer's group.

1. Water Buddy

When I was a little girl, I went to a day camp which consisted of two picnic tables and a lake. Everyone was assigned a water buddy. The water buddy was to keep you from drowning while the counselors had a smoke.

Every writer should have a water buddy. In my workshops, everyone gets one, whether they like it or not. Your water buddy reads your first draft, and your second. Your water buddy presents the piece to the workshop, putting in a good word for you and mentioning things that were difficult. The water buddy prevents you from changing tenses in the middle, from misspelling your protagonist's name, from writing sentences that will make you cringe a day later.

People often come to love their water buddies. It turns out that almost anyone is better than the writer at catching mistakes, fielding errant metaphors and seeing the writer's intention through the unfortunate sentence.

2. Portraits/Language Reveals Character

All the writers are divided into pairs, with people they don't know. The instruction is: talk to each other for twenty minutes. Write a portrait of the other person. The whole exercise takes forty minutes.

Each pair then reads, in turn. I encourage the group to listen for a number of things: some incidental but intriguing details (the two portraits so often seemed linked by language or by character or by details chosen) and to tone and inflection, the word choice, the details selected and the way these three things create a particular voice or character. The heart of this exercise is: There is nothing observed without an observer AND every single sentence reflects a point of view.

Students quickly see the way in which the writer has shaped the portrait, even unconsciously, and I encourage them to think of the portrait they are hearing as a portrait of the writer, as well as of the object. Sometimes, I will ask them to rewrite the portrait, with one change (you are former lovers and have not seen each other for a year; you are about to break up; she is terminally ill and has not been told). This leads to further attention to character and the interaction of story with character and language.

LISTENING TO SOUND TO FIND SENSE

Victoria Redel is a poet and fiction writer. Her most recent books are *Loverboy* and *Swoon*. *Loverboy* has been adapted for a film to be directed by Kevin Bacon. She teaches at Sarah Lawrence College and in the graduate program of Columbia University.

Way too often I find that I've tightened up as a writer, worrying about what should happen in the fiction—what a character or characters should do, how to move along the story—when in truth, I believe that how it happens, the language of the page, is the really essential concern. Despite not believing that plot is at the core or even much matters in fiction, I can find myself worrying and dead-ending up that path. It is through syntax, word choice, sentence making that I find the most useful possibilities of character and dramatic action.

I came to fiction first as a poet and in refocusing on the cadences and possibilities in language I return to my belief that there's no distinguishing between form and content in a work of art. To reorient myself to language and the rhythms of sentences, I try to fool around—sometimes within the story and sometimes as exercises (think playing scales or riffs with an instrument). There are really endless games I can play—and have happily found that they open up work that has seemed limited or constrained even deadened by the imposition of prior "ideas." Like all play there are rules. And

I've found that these rules wind up yielding surprise and freedom I would never have considered if I were working the "plot." I'm not saying that all or any of it makes its way into the finished work, but here are a few that have yielded wonderful results:

EXERCISES

1. Word Choice

Write a one- to three-page scene using only single-syllable words. Here having to work the language, or work around "what I want to say" to "how it must be said" provides some surprising linguistic gestures. I often throw in arbitrary words that have to be used—which makes me have to reach and create what happens by listening to and striving for language.

2. Sentence Making Short and Long

Write a scene using sentences made up of no more than five words per sentence. Again, what is interesting in this exercise is that what happens becomes integral or inseparable from how it is happening in language.

Then try to work a scene using sentences of real length and heft. Can I push the sentence to a big paragraph length? Notice the effect of such a sentence. Can I then meet that paragraph with another of even greater length? Here there's so much fun in really grasping the plasticity of the English sentence; honestly, this is how I learned grammar. What are the effects in a sentence of adverbial or adjectival clauses? What happens to the sound of the sentence when preposition phrases are piled up?

You can see that from here the possibilities expand: long and short sentences, then paragraph rules. What happens if a paragraph goes on for pages? Or, conversely, if single-sentence paragraphs are deployed?

ENTRANCES: BUILDING
BIGGER SCENES

Lynne Barrett is the author of two books of short stories, *The Secret Names of Women* and *The Land of Go*. Her stories have been anthologized in *A Dixie Christmas, Mondo Barbie, Simply the Best Mysteries*, and *Literature: Reading and Responding to Fiction, Poetry, Drama and the Essay*, among others. She wrote the libretto for a children's opera, *Cricketina*, and is coeditor of the anthology *Birth: A Literary Companion*. A recipient of the Edgar Award for best mystery short story and a National Endowment for the Arts Fellowship, she teaches in the MFA program at Florida International University.

I took a course in stage lighting in college and afterward sometimes operated the lighting for plays in the school's oldest auditorium. Working the Frankensteinesque switches, I would stand on a platform above the wings, downstage left, where I could see both the actors on stage and those waiting to enter. From my perch, I think I absorbed the dramatic importance of entrances, how all relationships can change when a new character is added to the mix.

In teaching, I have found that beginning fiction writers will often construct chains of short scenes with just one or two characters present. It's natural to do this; we are initially most comfortable writing a character alone, or that character in a series of one-on-one encounters. But memorable fiction offers the contrast of small private scenes with larger, public ones and makes dramatic use of entrances and exits. Watch Jane Austen bring her people together at the ball at Netherfield in *Pride and Prejudice,* spinning plots and subplots forward, or Henry James use entrances and discoveries in *The Ambassadors* to educate Strether in the ways of France or Fitzgerald send Nick Carroway through Gatsby's party in search of his host, and you see the pleasure that can be gained in setting an individual within larger groups and exploring the dramatic arc of a social situation.

But to be good at this, you need some practice. To gain confidence and learn more about characters and their relationships with one another, you can practice scenic construction, writing dialogue for varying numbers of characters and setting major characters against a crowd, so that when the occasion arises to do this in a story or novel you have the skills to pull it off.

The exercise sequence I offer here can build up a writer's scenic choices. The first step gives you a building block useful in all sorts of fiction, while the most complex works toward the big scenes or set pieces of a novel.

EXERCISE

You should work on these exercises over the course of several writing sessions, doing no more than one step each day. For steps 6 and 7 you may want to take longer:

1. Choose a setting where multiple characters would be present: a party, office, club—any location where people will be able to talk and hear one another. Start with two in dialogue. Bring in a third character. The dynamic between people should change with the entrance of this person. The entrance might be anticipated, or could be an interruption.

2. Have the three talk about a fourth character.

3. Then bring in the fourth character. Let the four talk.

4. Have two of them talk more privately (can be anything from a moment to a page) while the others are present but preoccupied with some activity.

5. Have one of the characters leave. Let the others discuss him or her.

6. Then, turn the exercise around: Take the setting and group you have been working with and this time start with the action going on inside but choose the point of view of a character outside who is about to enter. Establish your character outside and what he or she wants: give him/her someone he/she anticipates seeing and affecting. Then take your character into the scene and let your point-of-view character see, hear, notice the event as a whole (crowd, spectacle, sense details) and encounter individuals and groups. If you are using people you have already built in steps 1–5, you will be able to write about them with confidence and you will be aware that they are talking about more than your character may know, which creates a strong three-dimensional effect.

7. Think of a new setting to which you can take your characters, where even larger numbers would be. In considering entrances and exits, think about the phases of an event, whether a picnic, a bachelor party, or a funeral. Define subgroups when a larger cast is present, such as one table at a wedding reception. As you read, pay attention to how writers you admire are using these techniques.

THE FIVE SECOND SHORTCUT TO WRITING IN THE LYRIC REGISTER

Steve Almond is the author of two collections of short stories—*The Evil B. B. Chow and Other Stories* and *My Life in Heavy Metal*—and *Candyfreak: A Journey Through the Chocolate Underbelly of America.*. *Which Brings Me to You: A Novel in Confessions*, which Almond cowrote with the novelist Julianna Baggott, was published in the spring of 2006. Almond's stories have appeared in *Playboy*, *Tin House*, *Zoetrope: All-Story*, *The Virginia Quarterly Review*, *Ploughshares*, and other publications. His fiction has been included in New Stories from the South 2003, *Zoetrope: All-Story 2*, and *The Best American Erotica.* He is the winner of the 2002 Pushcart Prize and in 2001 he was a National Magazine Award finalist. He teaches creative writing at Boston College and at Grub Street, a Boston-based nonprofit creative-writing center.

M any young writers believe that if they throw enough beauty at the page, the result will be truth. In fact, just the opposite is true. The effort to express complex emotional truths with precision is what leads language to rise into beauty.

This exercise attempts to compel writers to slow down when the emotions are running highest. The result, hopefully, is a compression of sensual and psychological detail that elevates prose into the lyric register.

EXERCISE

1. Write a short scene that captures some intense moment from your life, such as your first kiss or the first time you were deeply ashamed or powerfully scared.

2. The bulk of the scene must take in *no more than five seconds.* That is: you should be writing about a very small segment of time.

3. Rather than moving the action forward, concentrate on slowing down and moving the action inward. The key here is to keep yourself from racing ahead. You must capture *everything* that is going on in this very short chronology.

4. This act of compression will help your writing rise into the lyric register, which is marked by a compression of sensual and psychological detail.

5. If you have a scene in a novel or story that feels too rushed, apply the above instructions. Isolate a single, five-second period and force yourself to record everything that is happening to the characters, both in the physical world around them and the emotional world within them.

CHRISTOPHER BUSA

MEANING MAKING VIA METAPHOR

Christopher Busa is the editor of *Provincetown Arts* magazine and of books published by the Provincetown Arts Press. His interviews and essays have appeared in *Arts, Garden Design, The Paris Review, Partisan Review,* and elsewhere. He is on the faculty of the graduate program in creative writing at Wilkes University in Wilkes-Barre, Pennsylvania.

When I consider if writing is good, I don't make a distinction between fiction and nonfiction. But I have found in my role as editor of *Provincetown Arts* that fiction must be ten times better than nonfiction for me to be persuaded to publish it. To write fiction is to persuade readers that an alternative reality is more compelling than conventional reality. A work of fiction that makes its way into the lifeblood of our culture usually possesses an uncanny echo of successive refinements in meaning, so that the world in the writing is built from the material detail of facts and the mortar of finding a way to make the pieces stick together. Like bridge building, some engineering is required for these transcendent traverses.

Metaphor is the mortar for the writer who would build her or his edifice to last, to endure as an imaginative conception. Making art is plastic and mysterious, yet artists are practical people who find concrete ways to accomplish their goals. It is said of Tintoretto, the Venetian artist who was dazzled in the day by the refracting light off the waters of the city's canals, that he arranged smoke, mirrors, and small wax models on a stage in his studio, which he could rotate, so that the same shapes could be seen from other angles. The idea is to spark metaphoric connections. The writer, likewise, strives to link word, image, and idea. A lively still life, like a lively piece of writing, is the product of a lively mind. A metaphor is like a bucket used to carry water, a device to conduct an action. Now, if action is the goal, we must ask what the purpose is, and here we discover that a piece of writing begins with a genuine question, provoking the writer to write. It almost doesn't matter where you begin, because your unconscious will lead you to your interest if you pursue the first question that comes to your mind unbidden.

Write down a question anchored in a noun. Examine the question and key word again and again, as if they are objects that have become malleable through the magic of naming. Expand upon your question, allowing it to divide, enlarge, and shrink into other shapes, realities, and truths, thinking how the gift of a nodal point is a seed for your imagination. A nagging feeling that you don't know something can identify a desire. Divide the question into parts, like a cook preparing the sequence of a recipe. It helps if now the question can be asked from two points of view, one specific and the other general: What is the function of a generator in a motorcycle engine? What is the meaning of life? Keep notes; your notes are hyperlinks to your unconscious. Your imagination will allow you to find a metaphorical connection between a pear and a peacock, or something even more interesting.

Here is an exercise that is helpful in creating metaphoric connections.

EXERCISE

Choose three key words that are resonant for you. Place each at the head of its own column and generate about twenty word associations for each key word. I might start as follows:

ROAD	TIME	SHOE
journey	bliss	sole
path	hunger	soul
goal	ice	aspire

Here you are at the mercy of your unconscious, which enjoys toying with you and may lead you down incongruous paths. Like a devoted suitor, be persistent; when one word is not right, try again. Draw lines connecting diverse words on your notebook page, and the page will evolve into clusters, suggesting some three-part organization. In my example, I could cluster *journey, hunger,* and *soul.* That is enough to create a group of metaphors to begin work. Three is about the number of factors, or metaphors, that a short piece of writing can carry, and a long piece of writing achieves unity in the same proportional expansion. A metaphor likening two disparate things will usually possess, at least implicitly, a third perspective. After all, somebody is doing the metaphor making, writing that balanced sentence that lofts, as on a seesaw, two weights balanced on the fulcrum of a purpose. Like energy, mass, and the speed of light, the dynamic metaphors that organize the thinking in a piece of writing must possess some of the accurate elements of a meaningful equation.

In his *Poetics* Aristotle said, "The greatest thing by far is to be a master of metaphor. It is the one thing that cannot be learned from others; it is a sign of genius because good metaphor means the eye catches resemblance." This exercise has made me mindful of the therapeutic value of metaphor making, and I suddenly remember a line of John Ashbery's that I read thirty years ago. The good metaphor dissolves "that last level of anxiety that melts in becoming, like miles under the pilgrim's feet." In a way that is real via the progress of doing, we are pilgrims as we embark on our journey as writers, and metaphors are road signs.

SOUNDTRACKING YOUR STORY

Christopher Castellani is the author of two novels, *A Kiss from Maddalena* and *The Saint of Lost Things*. He holds a master of fine arts in creative writing from Boston University and is the artistic director of Grub Street, Inc., a Boston-based nonprofit creative-writing center.

I'm not one of those writers who needs total silence in which to work. In fact, I prefer the din and human energy of a coffee shop or a train car. If the room is too quiet, I start to feel as though I'm back in study hall, or I hear voices in the low hum of my laptop.

Sometimes, though, too much background noise can be distracting, or at least too strong a contrast to the world of the scene I'm trying to create. At those times, I have difficulty hearing or seeing my characters, getting under their skin or into their hearts; I'm stuck for a direction the story should go, or a decision the character should make. I want to live as my character(s) for a while, but I'm too much in the world of the coffee shop or the train car to focus adequately on the world of fiction.

To remedy this, I like to add to the clamor.

EXERCISE

Put on headphones and listen to the music your characters might be listening to. If the story is set in the early 1980s, and the character is of a certain type, I'll put on The Cure. If the character is an Italian villager circa 1943, I'll put on songs s/he might have heard on the radio during that time and place.

Where do I get these songs? Part of the fun of researching a novel or story is discovering the music of the era and examining it for clues about the culture. Most libraries have collections of music from various countries and time periods, and all will allow you to borrow them or at least listen to them on headphones during a writing session on the premises.

I strongly suggest making sure that the story you are working on is set in a distinct time and place, and that you take some time to live in that world again for a while—not only through music, but through as many different forms of media as you can find. Even if it's a time you lived through, you may not remember all the details. Read the tabloid magazines of that year. Read journals and letters written by people like your characters. If possible, go to the town hall of the city in which your character lived, and look up deeds and wills and other records. These will give you a very specific assessment of how people lived and what mattered to them.

Soundtracking your writing experience, though, has a number of particularly striking effects.

First, it's a quick and powerful path to the empathy you are always striving for as a writer: you imagine yourself as your character responding to the lyrics or the emotion of the music; you wonder if the words or the situation in the song have some resonance in the character's life. While writing my first book, set in a small Italian village during World War II, I remember being enchanted by the song "La Piccinina," in which a young man watches the girl he loves—but can't have—through the window of a store. The longing expressed in the soaring vocals of the singer helped me to relate more emotionally to the character of Vito, who had his own unrequited love.

Second, soundtracking helps to infuse your sentences with a certain rhythm or cadence that is particular to the time period. And if the work is historical, you may also pick up on some slang expressions or colloquialisms you might not find in other media.

Third, given that many songs are narrative and tell a story, the lyrics can spark ideas for plot or shifts in character. In the wonderful songs of the Italian crooners of the 1950s, I found a rich mine of stories: men who wanted to move in with their mothers after they got married, women who longed for the Old Country, and Christmas traditions gone awry.

Often, the music I've listened to while writing has provided me with not only ideas but a sense that I am living through the experience with my characters. I feel more closely connected to them, and, consequently, less lonely. Given how solitary the act of writing can be, any trick to stave off loneliness is one I am happy to share and to receive.

ROBERT COHEN

NEGATIVE CAPABILITY

Robert Cohen is the author of three novels, *The Organ Builder, The Here and Now,* and *Inspired Sleep*, and a collection of stories, *The Varieties of Romantic Experience*. He has received a Whiting Writers' Award, a Guggenheim, a Lila Wallace–Reader's Digest Writers' Award, the Ribalow Prize, and a Pushcart Prize, and his work has appeared in a wide variety of publications, including *Harper's, GQ, The Paris Review, Atlantic Unbound*, and *Ploughshares*. He teaches at Middlebury College in Vermont.

Generally with novice fiction I find that the beginnings and middles of the story are more interesting and suggestive than the resolution—that the pressure of contrivance takes over toward the end, and often flattens the complexity, the strangeness and possibility, of what's been established earlier. Maybe this is because for intelligent young writers who are hot to trot, it's difficult to hold back, to resist sharing all their cleverness with the lucky reader. But cleverness can take us only so far; what's needed at a certain point is less of it, less cleverness, less knowingness, fewer answers and more questions and wallowing in doubt. This goes deeper than craft; it's a question of perception, of a kind of patient, double-minded empiricism we see in Chekhov, for instance. Chekhov's work is not about "knowing" something, but about apprehending two opposing things at once, and then probing, and relishing, and also bemoaning, the paradox. Hence his famous neutrality of tone, the difficulty of distinguishing comedy from tragedy, courage from cowardice.

Not that we should all write like Chekhov, of course. But a healthy dose of double-mindedness, an attention to the promiscuous duality that is our nature and the world's, can help us find our way through the thickets of possibility in our stories, can provide the dynamic tension that makes them possible. And perhaps even necessary.

All of which is rather difficult to talk about in the abstract, so one way to approach it is to try to make it experiential.

EXERCISE

Read the first four-fifths of a short short story aloud (I prefer one by Chekhov, "The Little Trick," the first ending of which is atrocious, though he revised it twelve years after publication and made it much, much better). Write an ending for it. You may want to work with a writing buddy, a writing group, or perhaps you are a teacher and would like to assign this to a class.

Compare your ending to Chekhov's first ending, and then to his second. This may help underscore the need for what Keats calls Negative Capability—"that is, when man is capable of being in uncertainties, mysteries, doubts, without any irritable reaching after facts and reason."

For a fiction writer, this means not letting the pressure to resolve a plot override the obligation to remain true to the complex situation you've established, and to the characters' temperaments. It means inhabiting the darkness of not-knowing where the story is going perhaps longer than is comfortable, and intuiting your way toward the light. If this is done well, you may find that your ending(s) are more or less in accord with Chekhov's revised one: that is, if you have remained true to the provocative mysteries of the story, there is only a limited number of endings possible, and of tonalities for that ending.

REVISION

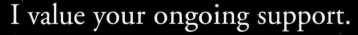

I value your ongoing support.

President Barack Obama cannot defeat the Republicans without your support of the DNC. Please help the DNC keep up the momentum for change.

Photo © Brooks Kraft/Corbis

PORTER SHREVE

SEVEN DRAFTS IN SEVEN DAYS

Porter Shreve is the author of three novels: *The Obituary Writer, Drives Like a Dream*, and *When the White House Was Ours* (forthcoming 2008). Coeditor of six anthologies, he directs the creative writing program at Purdue University.

When I heard in graduate school that Raymond Carver wrote as many as thirty drafts of his classic story "Cathedral," I thought about putting down my pen for good. I had never written more than two or three drafts of a short story, though I knew abstractly that revision is the key to making a story great. Widely anthologized short stories look easy because the language is so precise, the arc so perfectly paced and the ending inevitable, but it's important to remember that these narratives take most writers months, sometimes years, to compose.

How did Carver manage to find just the right word every time? How did he discover the particular voice of the unnamed narrator—down in the dumps but subtly yearning? In what ways did Carver's secondary characters—the wife and the blind man—push the narrator toward change? How did Carver happen upon the brilliant symbol of the Cathedral, a physical object on a television show that by the end of the story becomes a metaphor for the narrator's almost spiritual breakthrough? For Carver the answer rested in revision.

Ever since I learned this I've become a devoted reviser, and I encourage the same of my students.

In a workshop of anywhere from ten to twenty people it can be overwhelming to try to figure out whose critiques to take to heart. You pay particular attention to your instructor's comments, but you also want to take into account some of your fellow students' suggestions. But when you receive so much critique, some of it contradictory, it can be hard to stay focused or maintain the energy that first inspired you. So instead of doing the wholesale revisions that nearly all first drafts need, you might make only cursory changes, adding a sentence here, fixing a run-on there, perhaps changing the title. "This isn't a revision," your instructor says, and you feel frustrated, misunderstood, perhaps shortsightedly defiant. Writers working on their own have a different but equally daunting challenge. Without outside voices telling them "cut this" or "add that," one is often left wondering where to begin.

Revision doesn't need to feel like a chore. For many writers, the pleasure is not in getting the first draft on the page but in rearranging the puzzle until all the pieces fit. This exercise will give you an opportunity to write many drafts in a relatively short space of time. With any luck you'll clear the revision hurdle and feel that with each draft you're making your story clearer, better and deeper.

EXERCISE

You're going to be writing seven drafts of your story, but instead of trying to take all the problems into account at once you're going to focus in each draft on a different element of fiction. I'd recommend the following order, but you should feel free to choose your own:

Draft one: Character

Draft two: Conflict

Draft three: Setting

Draft four: Voice and Point of View

Draft five: Plot and Structure

Draft six: Language

Draft seven: Symbol

On each day you should underline your workshop's, your first reader's or your own comments according to the given subject. On day one, for example, underline anything pertaining to character; on day five, underline anything having to do with plot and structure. On each day focus exclusively on the particular element assigned to that draft. If your story seems to need a more evocative sense of place, look for sections where you can use sensory details to describe the physical aspects of a particular environment. Where on day five you'd focus on the big picture—the chronology of events as they apply to plot and structure—on days six and seven you'd narrow in on sharpening your language sentence to sentence and giving the symbols or potential symbols in your story greater shape and clarity.

Often you'll find at the end of a given day that the process of revision has just begun. If you have time, you should by all means spend more than one day before moving on to the next element of fiction. If you move on, though, you should do so with the knowledge that you'll probably have to return and spend more days on certain problem areas. Perhaps, for example, you were able to make the protagonist fuller on day one of your revisions, but you still need to flesh out one or more secondary characters. If you think of a story as a living text you'll feel freer to re-imagine and rewrite it until all the various parts are in place and working simultaneously.

MORE IS MORE: AN EXERCISE IN REVISING YOUR STORY

Ann Harleman is the author of *Happiness*, a collection of short stories that won the Iowa Short Fiction Award, and *Bitter Lake*, a novel. Among her awards are Guggenheim and Rockefeller fellowships, two Rhode Island State Arts Council grants, the Berlin Prize in Literature, the PEN Syndicated Fiction Award, the O. Henry Award, and a Rona Jaffe Foundation Writers' Award. She is on the faculties of Brown University and the Rhode Island School of Design.

Revising, I tell my students, is four-fifths of the creative process. It's the most painful and the most pleasurable aspect of writing. Painful, because you have to destroy a fair amount of your own prose; pleasurable, because through successive revisions you see your story take shape.

There are two ways to approach revision: paring down and expanding. Paring Down is often the one that comes to mind first. Think of Ezra Pound's drastic compression of "The Wasteland," or Elmore Leonard's advice to leave out the parts that people skip. And the maxim famous among writers, "Kill your darlings!"—variously credited to Flaubert, Nabokov, and Faulkner—advocates Paring Down with a vengeance.

Expanding is trickier. It's a matter of going deeper, so that your story is more fully and truly imagined. Brenda Ueland (*If You Want to Write*) put it best: "Do not try to think of better *words*. Try to see the people better. . . . See them—just what they did and how they looked and felt." Plot, character, setting, description, dialogue, point of view—in Expanding, all the elements of fiction come into play, in a way that's different for every story.

Discussions of revising often restrict themselves to Paring Down, because this approach lends itself more easily to formulas. But I've found it best, in dealing with both my own writing and that of my students, to Expand first, and Pare Down afterward. It's easier to see what doesn't belong when you know what does. If you can see the *Yes* behind the *No,* you'll be much happier committing all the little murders that rewriting demands. Revision will feel more like Michelangelo's process of finding the figure hidden inside the block of marble. The difference between writers and sculptors is that we have to generate our own marble. Expanding does this by increasing the depth and breadth of your initial draft. Inside this larger swath lurks your story. More often than not, it's different from the story you first sat down to write.

Here, then, is an exercise to help you re-see your story.

EXERCISE

Step One: Quarry

Remember, the goal is to go deeper into what you've already written. You're going to reread your draft and let it speak to you, looking for the opportunities it offers.

First, make a list of the nouns, verbs, and adjectives that are repeated. Do you see themes or ideas in this list? Images? Atmosphere? Jot down what you see, without using your original vision of the story to interpret or clarify. The two lists, combined, are your Touchstone List. Lean back, close your eyes, and take a few minutes just to hold the list in your mind. If more words or images come, let them; but don't write them down.

Now go back to your draft again. Take a highlighter and mark the spots where you feel excitement. Then mark the spots where you feel confusion, where there's something you don't understand (When we're not sure, Graham Greene said, that's when we are alive). Finally, mark the spots where you feel despair—where the prose doesn't work, and you don't think you can make it work.

These spots are your first draft's gifts to you. They are the points where you can dig down into your story and re-imagine it. Take them in the order they come in, one by one. With respect to each spot, first reread your Touchstone List, just to refresh it in your mind. Then ask yourself, with respect to the particular passage you're working on, What can we see? What can we hear? What can we touch? Taste? Smell? Finally, ask yourself, What's in motion? (Characters, objects, landscape, weather—you name it.) I call this the Six Senses Scan. Now write a second draft of the passage. Move on to the next spot and the next, until you've gone all the way through your draft.

By the time you're done, your story will have lengthened, widened, deepened—and, if you're lucky, changed. This second draft will be messier; but it will be richer. Now take it and repeat the whole process. Keep repeating it until you feel that small, internal click that says, *Enough!* The one that tells you your marble is all there.

Step Two: Find the Spine

Inside your expanded draft your story waits. It's not the story you set out to write; so you let go of that. Now you need to look for the spine, the backbone, of your real story.

There's no formula for this. But you probably have—after the time and energy and imagination you invested in Step One—an instinctive grasp of your story's Central Thing. (If you don't, this is where a workshop or a writers' group or a single trusted reader can be useful. Ask them!) It might be an image or an object, or something a character thinks or feels, or an exchange between characters, or—well, anything at all! Put that Central Thing in a position of prominence—beginning, end, climax—whatever feels right.

Now you need to find, within your expanded draft, the shape that fits your new understanding of your story's center. This shape will be your story's spine; it will emerge as you go. The method I've found most useful is actual physical re-arranging. Cut up the draft into scenes (or sections, if scenes won't work). Try different sequences. Keep asking, with respect to each chunk, how does this connect to the spine? If you're not sure, but you feel that it might, put it to one side of the emerging spine. If it just plain doesn't, put it in a folder marked "Some Other Day."

You are now on the threshold of Paring Down. When you start to do so, you'll do it with the positive orientation you've established so firmly, asking—of each scene, each paragraph, each sentence, each word in a sentence—how does this connect to the spine? How does it serve the story? Because of the Expanding you've done, your story is now so real and vivid to you that it's become its own animal. It's no longer a spin-off of your ego, yet, at the same time, you've invested so much of yourself in it. The last thing you want to do is stand in its way.

BRIAN KITELEY

POTHOLES

Brian Kiteley is the author of the novels *Still Life with Insects* and *I Know Many Songs, but I Cannot Sing*, and the book of fiction exercises *The 3 A.M. Epiphany*. He directs the Ph.D. program in creative writing at the University of Denver.

I s it useful for writers to test their readers' skills at making illogical leaps from sentence to sentence or paragraph to paragraph? What usually happens between sentences or ellipses or chapters in stories? Writers should train themselves to leave out as much as they put into a story and to manipulate (in a sense) what they leave out—letting the absent material poke the story in the side so readers get a greater sense of the story below the story, than the surface narrative.

Life is full of stuff below the surface of reality—it's often called The Past. Narrative ought to have a pretty surface, but it can also be like a frozen pond you're walking along with your high school boyfriend—all squeezes, sighs, and meaningful glances, until you come across your boyfriend's identical twin brother below the ice staring up at you, arms spread out imploringly, the word "C-c-cold" clearly frozen on his dead lips. Meaning is often created by the logical gaps in our fiction.

In my own fiction I fight the urge to construct smooth and flowing narrations, because I think that smoothness is a vanity, a distortion of the story's reality. All writers think they're realists (no matter their literary political leanings), but writers may understand from this exercise that meaning is also produced off-stage, by the light technicians, the costume people, the guy who operates the trap door and elevators out of sight of the audience.

EXERCISE

Take six hundred words of one of your own old failed stories, only six hundred words. The first rule of this exercise is to train you to choose the tastiest part of an unsuccessful story. When you've given up on a story and don't have anything to lose, you should start taking chances, making bold moves you wouldn't otherwise attempt.

The second rule of the exercise is to eliminate two of every three sentences throughout the fragment (leaving one sentence standing). You do not need to cut the second of three sentences each time, for example. Remove any one of the three sentences from each three-sentence block. What's left will likely be difficult to understand. But you may feel a pattern of sense nevertheless pulses (narrative threads often remain even after great damage to the narrative).

The third rule of this exercise is that you can only add sentences or phrases; you can't rearrange the original order of your cut-up story.

The fourth and last rule of this exercise is that you should try to keep the feeling of sentences and even paragraphs missing between all the sentences of the final draft. These missing sentences and paragraphs don't need to be obvious, but they should be tangible. Efficient storytelling is all about leaving out unnecessary steps.

"The wedding was curt and almost entirely without result. At no point during the ceremony did the minister let anybody but himself be the center of attention. The halfway-decent thing about the reception was that the tables were so narrow, the guests could sit on only one side." This is Gary Lutz, 60 percent of his tiny story "Being Good in October," from his collection *Stories in the Worst Way.* What has happened between these sentences? Between the first and second sentences, there is a tenuous connection—the egotistical minister. Or was the minister simply doing what ministers do—*preside* over a wedding? Between the second and third sentences, the focus shifts away from the minister and the wedding to the guests (and the most important guest of all, the unseen narrator of these events, who never really reveals herself).

The final product of this exercise should be no more than six hundred words—you'll be adding back the equivalent of the material you cut in the first place.

THE DARK MATTER: TWENTY ISSUES IN NOVEL REVISION

A Nebraska native, Jonis Agee is the author of ten books, including most recently the collection of new and selected stories *Acts of Love on Indigo Road* and the novels *Sweet Eyes* and *The Weight of Dreams*. Her stories and essays have appeared in *The Iowa Review, Colorado Review*, and elsewhere. She's been awarded a National Endowment for the Arts Fellowship, two Loft-McKnight Fellowships for fiction, two Minnesota State Arts Board grants in fiction, and the Nebraska Book Award. Three of her books, *Strange Angels, Bend This Heart*, and *Sweet Eyes*, were named Notable Books of the Year by *The New York Times*. She teaches creative writing at the University of Nebraska–Lincoln and is director of the Nebraska Summer Writers' Conference.

Astronomers know that most of the universe exists in a dark, invisible form . . . dark matter provides the gravitational tugs that keep what astronomers can see in motion.

EXERCISE

1. The Missing Scene: What's missing that needs to be dramatized? Is there a scene referred to or summarized that isn't here? Is there a scene taking place in flashback that needs to

be moved forward into the on-going present of the novel? Have we spent the last fifty pages building up the big moment and you skip over it?

2. The Unnecessary Scene: the one we like so much for our own private reasons, but which does nothing to forward the dramatic momentum or thematic or emotional issues of the novel. It doesn't tell us anything new or important about the characters. It's our own doll baby.

3. It Sounds Familiar: character types, character issues, motivations, key events that have been done to death in the contemporary marketplace of ideas and popular concerns. If it's been on *Oprah* and *Montel Williams* and the best-seller list and in the newspapers and magazines and you have two friends or relatives with the same issue—stick a fork in it; it's done.

4. Holding Yourself Off: the problem of the middle ground. This can occur in the language, style, action, or character, especially the character when we hold her/him at arm's length. Ask why and then move closer. Don't be so darn careful and socially acceptable. Nothing happens in neutral—the car and the novel go nowhere except roll downhill.

5. Writing with Passion: This solves number four, and is done by writing through your body/your senses. Remember, what you are passionate about will lend passion to your writing which in turn transfers to the reader. Take a chance with passion, the edge; make us feel something, react to something.

6. Trusting the Reader: I'm not stupid—You're not stupid. You don't have to overexplain every piece of information or dialogue or theme or character. Let the characters talk and

move without you hovering over them. The pleasure for the reader occurs in watching the story unfold, following the characters through their lives, and figuring out what it means. Too much explaining saps emotion. If you can't move the reader, the book won't sell.

7. Writing Forward: Write each draft to the end. Don't, keep, stopping, and, going, back, to, correct, if, you, know, what, I, mean. In a novel, especially, you will get stuck with the first few chapters if you don't just write through the draft. And don't stop each chapter to perfect it, or each page, or each paragraph, or each sentence. You need to get the sweep, the scope of the novel through a couple of drafts before the final clean-up drafts. It will probably take you at least three to five drafts. Plan on more. Keep a pad of paper beside you and jot down the brilliant new ideas and changes you'll make on the next draft while you plow forward.

8. Why Don't They Like My Characters? Characters need to be people we are sympathetic to or interested in or both. If you're too nice or too mean to them, and if they're too nice or too rotten, we don't care. Roughen or lighten your characters. There are few true monsters. There are few true saints. Humans are a mixture of both, with one generally predominant. On the other hand, don't overly punish or protect your characters either. Let characters have a range of emotions. Everybody is passionate about something in his/her life, even if it's getting the postage stamp positioned correctly on the envelope. Work against type. No emerald-eyed women unless they're on invading spaceships.

9. Heat: Beginnings need problems and conflicts so we can feel the temperature already rising in your characters' lives.

The coals beneath the ashes can rekindle at any moment: fresh wood on the fire and a good stir make a blaze; everything changes shape when subjected to enough heat.

10. Landing the Dramatic Arc: When you look at the structure of your novel, you need to arrange events so that they build and crest and resolve at the end. After the crisis and resolution, the novel ends. Say good-bye. Don't keep writing because you want to see how your characters get along in the Promised Land. Stories build around problems and how humans solve them, not how they get along without problems. There's no mystery there.

11. Flashbacks Keep Calling Me: Go through and examine where they are. Make a list. Look at their length. When and where do they occur? Why are they there? Do you need them or should some of this material come forward into the dramatic present? Often the flashback is something we write for our own sake, to discover the character and the history of the world we're creating. Which flashback can be reduced to a sentence, a phrase, erased altogether? Sometimes we slip into flashback as a way of avoiding the present moment when we're stumped. Use them with care. They can impede the forward motion, the pacing, and momentum of the story.

12. The Closed World: One of the ways in which we can open the world of the novel, the lives of characters and sense of place and time is to embed facts and information in the narrative. Remember, we learn from reading novels. We like to take on worlds. Open yours. Take on more authority in the narrative.

13. Hello, I'm a Monologist: The problem of the first person who won't permit any other character, event, place, etc., room on the page is a normal stage in writing this narrative

form. Use action, dialogue, descriptions without the word *I* in them as often as possible. In fact, go through and see how much you can release from the death grip of the first person. The narrator doesn't have to give opinions and attitudes and emotions and reactions about every single thing that happens. Don't forget that as narrator, the person is telling a story. So make him do his job.

14. Hello, I'm in Love with My Own Voice: This is the third-person monologist who can't stop listening to his own big ideas and opinions and attitudes and reactions. Again. Tell the story. None of us are that darn fascinating. Imagine sitting next to this narrator in a plane on an O'Hare Airport runway for forty-five minutes in the middle of a heat wave on a July afternoon. That's your reader listening. That's you talking. Just tell the story.

15. Unload the Plot: Relax. You can use at least fifteen of those extra strands in your next five books. Often we overcomplicate the plot lines out of fear: fear that our writing and language aren't good enough so if we add a lot of extras, no one will notice; fear that our characters are flat and simple, but if we force them to act like Einstein in a labyrinth of events, no one will notice; fear that we really have nothing to say; fear that our story isn't interesting enough so we jazz it up with lots of extras. Listen, the best hamburger is the one with meat you can still taste despite the condiments.

16. Home, Sweet Home: Can my readers find the place I'm writing about on a map? Even if it's invented, can they locate the streets and buildings and landscape by the plants and animals and rocks and contours of the land? Do they know the economics and weather of the place? Will they be able to walk around the inside of my characters' houses,

rooms, workplaces in the dark without hurting themselves because they pretty much know where everything is?

17. He's Not Heavy, He's My Character: Can my reader see/ identify each character by some significant physical attributes? Are my characters shown in action, at work, physically engaged in something? Do we spend as much time outside the characters as inside their heads? Even more outside than inside?

18. Final Exam: Is each scene and chapter contributing directly to the forward motion of the novel? Are events located in specific time so my reader doesn't stumble around in confusion? Have I distinguished between flashback and dramatic present? Have I stayed with the narrative point of view I chose in the beginning? Do I need all the focal characters or should I stick with a few main ones? Is each scene given/ told from the focus of the appropriate character? Are there stereotypes and clichés I could change if I weren't too tired? Are there characters and scenes I have never been able to achieve?

19. Now Put It Aside for a Week to a Month: At the end of this time, pick it up and reread it with a dispassionate eye— you'll know this eye because it neither loves nor loathes. It can see where the strength of the book is and where the weakness is. Have the courage to revise again, or the courage to start sending it out. You'll know which you need to do when you reread. If in doubt, give it to someone else to read. It doesn't hurt to let a book sit a bit and season. We're not talking years, of course.

20. The Lesson Endeth: Go forth and write and write and write and write. Then revise.

AUTHOR WEB SITES

Chris Abani **www.chrisabani.com**

Diana Abu-Jaber **www.dianaabujaber.com**

Jonis Agee **http:mockingbird.creighton.edu/NCW/agee.htm**

Steve Almond **www.stevenalmond.com**

Tony Ardizzone **http:www.indiana.edu/~girgenti/**

Thomas Fox Averill **http:www.washburn.edu/cas/english/taverill**

Lynne Barrett **www.lynnebarrett.com**

Douglas Bauer **www.douglasbauer.org**

Karen Bender **www.uncw.edu/writers/faculty-benderk.html**

Venise Berry **www.veniseberry.com**

Robert Boswell **www.robertboswell.com**

Amy Bloom **www.amybloom.com**

Christopher Busa **www.provincetownarts.org**

Tania Casselle **www.tcwriter.com**

Christopher Castellani **www.chriscastellani.com**

Alexander Chee **http:truenorth.typepad.com/fictioneer**

K. L. Cook **www.klcook.net.**

Clyde Edgerton **www.clydedgerton.com**

Cai Emmons **www.caiemmons.com**

Laurie Foos **www.lauriefoos.com.**

Kirby Gann **www.kirbygann.net.**

Sands Hall **www.sandshall.com**

Ann Harleman **http:faculty.risd.edu/faculty/aharlema/**

Michelle Herman **www.michelleherman.com**

Bret Anthony Johnston **www.bretanthonyjohnston.com**

Brian Kiteley **www.du.edu/~bkiteley/advice.html**

Sheila Kohler **www.sheilakohler.com**

Paul Lisicky **www.paullisicky.com**

Alison Lurie **http:people.cornell.edu/pages/al28/**

Renée Manfredi **www.reneemanfredi.com**

Edie Meidav **www.ediemeidav.com**

Sean Murphy **www.murphyzen.com**

Jayne Anne Phillips **www.jayneannephillips.com**

Robert Anthony Siegel **www.uncw.edu/writers/faculty-siegelr.html**

Leslie Schwartz **www.leslieschwartz.com**

Sandra Scofield **www.sandrascofield.com**

Porter Shreve **www.portershreve.com**

John Smolens **www.johnsmolens.com**

Debra Spark **www.colby.edu/personal/d/daspark/publications.html**

Susan Vreeland **www.svreeland.com**

Dan Wakefield **www.danwakefield.com**

Crystal Wilkinson **www.crystalwilkinson.com**

ACKNOWLEDGMENTS

Thanks to my editor, Ashley Shelby, and to my agent, Jenoyne Adams, for all their support and guidance; to all the writers who generously contributed a writing exercise for this anthology; to my husband, Francis Ellis; my mother, Jeannette Sokoloff; and my friends Maeve Moses, Lynn St. Clair, Edward Cabral, Fran Harrison, Bill Spielman, Sharon O'Halloran, Laurie Porter, and Rita Marko, who have always encouraged me.

CREDITS

ABOUT THE EDITOR

SHERRY ELLIS became interested in developing this anthology of writing exercises after she attended several writing workshops in which writing exercises were employed. Her author interviews have appeared in *The Kenyon Review, Glimmer Train,* and *AGNI,* as well as other literary and arts magazines. Ms. Ellis is at work on a collection of author interviews and a novel. She teaches writing at a community education program in Concord, Massachusetts, and provides individual coaching to writers.

Merle Haggard was sent to
San Quentin when he was
19 - - -